PRESIDENT'S MALARIA INITIATIVE

Benin

Malaria Operational Plan FY 2016

TABLE OF CONTENTS

ABBREVIATIONS and ACRONYMS

ACT	Artemisinin-based combination therapy
AL	Artemether-lumefantrine
ANC	Antenatal care
ARM3	Accelerating the Reduction of Malaria Morbidity and Mortality
AS/AQ	Artesunate-amodiaquine
BCC	Behavioral change communication
CAME	Central Medical Stores
CBAC	Benin Business Coalition against HIV, TB and Malaria
CDC	Centers for Disease Control and Prevention
CHW	Community health worker
CREC	*Centre de Recherche Entomologique de Cotonou*
DHS	Demographic and Health Survey
DSME	National Directorate for Maternal and Child Health
DTS	Dried tube specimen
EPI	Expanded program on immunization
ETAT	Emergency triage assessment and treatment
EUV	End-use verification survey
FY	Fiscal year
Global Fund	Global Fund to Fight AIDS, Tuberculosis and Malaria
GHI	Global Health Initiative
GOB	Government of Benin
HMIS	Health management information system
HSS	Health systems strengthening
iCCM	Integrated community case management
IMCI	Integrated management of childhood illness
IPTp	Intermittent preventive treatment for pregnant women
IRS	Indoor residual spraying
ITN	Insecticide-treated net
LEADD	Leadership and Development
LMIS	Logistics Management and Information System
LMU	Logistics Management Unit
M&E	Monitoring and evaluation
MICS	Multi-Indicator Cluster Survey
MIP	Malaria in pregnancy
MIS	Malaria Indicator Survey
MOH	Ministry of Health
MOP	Malaria operational plan
NGO	Non-governmental organization
NMCP	National Malaria Control Program
NSP	National Strategic Plan
OP	Organophosphate
OR	Operational research
OTSS	Outreach Training and Supportive Supervision
PBF	Performance-based financing
PCV	Peace Corps Volunteer
PMI	President's Malaria Initiative

RAMU	*Régime d'Assurance Maladie Universelle*
RBM	Roll Back Malaria
RDT	Rapid diagnostic test
RMIS	Routine Malaria Information System
SIAPS	System for Improved Pharmaceutical Services
SP	Sulfadoxine-pyrimethamine
SSFFC	Sub-standard, spurious, falsified, falsely-labeled, and counterfeit drugs
TWG	Technical Working Group
UNICEF	United Nations Children's Fund
USAID	United States Agency for International Development
USG	United States Government
USP PQM	United Stated Pharmacopeia Pharmaceutical Quality Management
WHO	World Health Organization
WHOPES	WHO Pesticide Evaluation Scheme

I. EXECUTIVE SUMMARY

When it was launched in 2005, the goal of the President's Malaria Initiative (PMI) was to reduce malaria-related mortality by 50% across 15 high-burden countries in sub-Saharan Africa through a rapid scale-up of four proven and highly effective malaria prevention and treatment measures: insecticide-treated mosquito nets (ITNs); indoor residual spraying (IRS); accurate diagnosis and prompt treatment with artemisinin-based combination therapies (ACTs); and intermittent preventive treatment for pregnant women (IPTp). With the passage of the Tom Lantos and Henry J. Hyde Global Leadership against HIV/AIDS, Tuberculosis, and Malaria Act in 2008, PMI developed a U.S. Government Malaria Strategy for 2009–2014. This strategy included a long-term vision for malaria control in which sustained high coverage with malaria prevention and treatment interventions would progressively lead to malaria-free zones in Africa, with the ultimate goal of worldwide malaria eradication by 2040-2050. Consistent with this strategy and the increase in annual appropriations supporting PMI, four new sub-Saharan African countries and one regional program in the Greater Mekong Subregion of Southeast Asia were added in 2011. The contributions of PMI, together with those of other partners, have led to dramatic improvements in the coverage of malaria control interventions in PMI-supported countries, and all 15 original countries have documented substantial declines in all-cause mortality rates among children less than five years of age.

In 2015, PMI launched the next six-year strategy, setting forth a bold and ambitious goal with specific objectives. The PMI Strategy for 2015-2020 takes into account the progress over the past decade and the new challenges that have arisen. Malaria prevention and control remains a major U.S. foreign assistance objective and PMI's Strategy fully aligns with the U.S. Government's vision of ending preventable child and maternal deaths and ending extreme poverty. It is also in line with the goals articulated in the RBM Partnership's second global malaria action plan, *Action and Investment to defeat Malaria (AIM) 2016-2030: for a Malaria-free World* and WHO's updated *Global Technical Strategy 2016-2030*. Under the PMI Strategy 2015-2020, the U.S. Government's goal is to work with PMI-supported countries and partners to further reduce malaria deaths and substantially decrease malaria morbidity, towards the long-term goal of elimination.

Benin was selected as a PMI focus country in fiscal year (FY) 2007.

This FY 2016 Malaria Operational Plan (MOP) presents a detailed implementation plan for Benin based on the strategies of PMI and the National Malaria Control Program (NMCP). It was developed in consultation with the NMCP and with the participation of national and international partners involved in malaria prevention and control in the country. The activities that PMI is proposing to support fit in well with the National Malaria Control strategy and plan and build on investments made by PMI and other partners to improve and expand malaria-related services, including the Global Fund to Fight AIDS, Tuberculosis, and Malaria (Global Fund) malaria grants. This document briefly reviews the current status of malaria control policies and interventions in Benin, describes progress to date, and identifies challenges and unmet needs to achieving the targets of the NMCP and PMI, and provides a description of activities that are planned with FY 2016 funding.

The proposed FY 2016 PMI budget for Benin is $16.5 million. PMI will support the following intervention areas with these funds:

Insecticide-treated nets (ITNs): The NMCP's Strategic Plan (2011-2018) promotes the provision of ITNs through two main delivery channels: universal coverage campaigns every three years and routine service delivery. PMI contributed to the 2014 universal net campaign through the procurement and distribution of 680,000 nets. Fiscal year 2015 PMI support includes the routine distribution of 730,000 nets for antenatal care (ANC) and the expanded program on immunization (EPI) services offered in public health facilities. Using FY 2016 resources, PMI will procure and distribute 520,000 long-lasting insecticide-treated nets (ITNs) to health facilities for routine distribution to pregnant women and children under five years of age. PMI will also procure and pre-position an estimated 1,000,000 ITNs for the 2017 universal net campaign. With an estimated 6.1 million nets needed for the 2017 national campaign, at the time of writing this MOP, there remains a 680,000 net gap after PMI and other donor support. PMI will continue to work with the Global Fund and the Government of Benin (GOB) to find ways to meet this need through reviewing net size specifications, additional support, or modified coverage strategies that still provide protection to the most vulnerable populations.

Indoor residual spraying (IRS): While an integral component of the National Malaria Strategic Plan, implementation of IRS in Benin is limited as PMI is the sole donor supporting the intervention. The 2015 spray round targets nine communes (~252,000 structures, population ~800,000) in the department of Atacora, which has a seasonal malaria transmission pattern. Recent monitoring results suggest that in some areas of Atacora, perennial transmission is more present than previously assumed. Since 2014, PMI has supported capacity building of the NMCP to play a greater role in the planning and implementation of IRS. In 2015, the NMCP increased its IRS implementation area from one to three communes. However, funding for the IRS campaign will be reduced temporarily in 2017, affecting the number of communes to be covered. Given limited resources and to maximize the public health impact of IRS, PMI will convene the national vector control partners to reassess current approaches and determine a short, medium, and long-term plan for the future of IRS in Benin. With FY 2016 funds, PMI will support the implementation of the new plan's road map for IRS implementation and insecticide resistance monitoring within the context of continued local capacity building among the NMCP, the *Centre de Recherche Entomologique de Cotonou* (CREC), and the National University of Abomey-Calavi.

Malaria in pregnancy (MIP): The national guidelines for IPTp are aligned now with the new WHO standards of monthly SP treatment beginning early in the second trimester of pregnancy up until delivery. During the last 12-18 months, PMI trained 608 health professionals and 1,214 community health workers (CHWs) on MIP. Further, PMI procured more than 1.5 million treatments of SP, distributed 470,000 ITNs to ANC clinics, and trained 1,043 health workers in order to enhance the provision of effective MIP services in public health facilities in Benin. While IPTp2 coverage has improved from 3% to 23% according to the 2006 and 2011-2012 DHS, and has reached 43% according to the 2014 national RMIS reports, it still falls short of the PMI and NMCP targets of 85% and 100% respectively. To accelerate SP coverage, PMI will reinforce behavior change training and messaging to improve the demand for IPTp services and improve service delivery performance among health workers in the public and private sectors.

Case management: The national case management guidelines recommend universal diagnostic testing for malaria by all health workers, and mandate free rapid diagnostic tests and treatment by public providers and CHWs for children under five years of age and pregnant women. In 2014, the NMCP completed updates to the national case management guidelines to align with the WHO recommendation for IPTp treatments and the treatment of severe malaria with injectable artesunate. PMI continues to support a comprehensive diagnostics and treatment program that involves the training of health workers and laboratory technicians, the implementation of a quality control and quality assurance system, strengthening supervision to ensure that health workers follow clinical practice guidelines, and provision of diagnostic and treatment commodities such as rapid diagnostic tests (RDTs) and artemisinin-based combination therapies (ACTs). Training of CHWs nationwide on RDTs as part of integrated community case management (iCCM) was recently completed. To maintain this progress, PMI supports both pre-

and in-service training for health workers nationwide. Scaling up training and access to malaria commodities for private sector health care providers is still underway.

Health systems strengthening and capacity building (HSS): Benin's health system continues to receive support from major health donors including PMI. This support focuses on major areas such as building the capacity of the health system to coordinate malaria interventions as well as supporting maternal and child health. However, despite progress shown in malaria indicators as evidenced by 2011-2012 Demographic and Health Survey (DHS) data, the NMCP continues to face major challenges in coordinating malaria control activities. To support the NMCP in addressing these challenges, PMI continues to invest in the support of in-country Technical Working Group (TWG) teams designed to provide technical expertise to the NMCP to make sound and informed policy decisions. PMI's support for reforming the Central Medical Stores (CAME) and commodities distribution since its inception in FY 2008 has started paying off with an improved governance of CAME and a clear vision articulated in the development plan of the institution which paves the way for significant reduction in stockouts. With FY 2016 resources, PMI will continue supporting reform of the supply chain in order to support commodities management and distribution at the decentralized level. Support to the Routine Malaria Information System (RMIS) will continue to enable the NMCP to collect and process data for decision-making. While not directly funding performance-based financing (PBF), PMI will continue to support complementary HSS approaches that enable health managers to improve malaria performance.

Behavior change communication (BCC): The NMCP has developed a new integrated communication plan that includes strategies for advocacy, BCC, and social mobilization. As part of the process, PMI supported a literature review to identify barriers to the use of IPTp, ITNs, and care-seeking for sick children. Strategic studies are underway to develop messages for improving the repair and maintenance of ITNs and for accepting RDTs at the community level. With FY 2016 funding, PMI will support the application of the strategies detailed in the integrated communication plan and the national malaria BCC plan by local community health organizations and the MOH. With heightened concern over and concrete evidence surfacing regarding the presence of sub-standard, spurious, falsified, falsely-labeled, and counterfeit (SSFFC) ACTs in the marketplace, PMI continues to support special communication campaigns targeting urban populations to discourage purchasing fake ACTs from informal vendors given the potential for dangerous health consequences.

Monitoring and evaluation (M&E): PMI has contributed to strengthening Benin's M&E systems, and the number of health facilities reporting timely and complete data to the health management information system (HMIS) has significantly increased. In past years, PMI has supported two national-level household surveys to provide information on key malaria indicators (the 2006 and 2011-2012 DHS). In 2009 and 2013, health facility surveys were conducted to assess the quality of malaria case management. With FY 2016 funding, PMI will continue providing technical guidance and financial support to strengthen the quality of routine malaria data collected, and continue to help build the NMCP's capacity to monitor and evaluate variations in morbidity and mortality and their relevance for ongoing programmatic activities. Support from PMI will contribute to key data collection and analysis activities, including quarterly end-use verification surveys (EUVs), the next DHS, currently planned for 2018, and work towards strengthening the NMCP's M&E strategy. PMI will also provide support for an impact evaluation of PMI interventions on all-cause child mortality indicators in Benin.

Operational research (OR): Since 2008, Benin has conducted multiple OR studies. Results from these studies have demonstrated the efficacy of IRS with non-pyrethroid-class insecticides on entomologic measures of malaria transmission, identified a colorimetric field test as an accurate and easier-to-use alternative to the standard bioassay for assessing ITN bio-efficacy, and quantified the serviceable life of

ITNs in the field to inform the timing of distribution and replacement. During 2014, PMI supported a study to demonstrate the feasibility of using dried tube specimens for field monitoring of RDT quality. No additional OR is planned with FY 2016 funding.

II. STRATEGY

1. Introduction

When it was launched in 2005, the goal of PMI was to reduce malaria-related mortality by 50% across 15 high-burden countries in sub-Saharan Africa through a rapid scale-up of four proven and highly effective malaria prevention and treatment measures: insecticide-treated mosquito nets (ITNs); indoor residual spraying (IRS); accurate diagnosis and prompt treatment with artemisinin-based combination therapies (ACTs); and intermittent preventive treatment for pregnant women (IPTp). With the passage of the Tom Lantos and Henry J. Hyde Global Leadership against HIV/AIDS, Tuberculosis, and Malaria Act in 2008, PMI developed a U.S. Government Malaria Strategy for 2009–2014. This strategy included a long-term vision for malaria control in which sustained high coverage with malaria prevention and treatment interventions would progressively lead to malaria-free zones in Africa, with the ultimate goal of worldwide malaria eradication by 2040-2050. Consistent with this strategy and the increase in annual appropriations supporting PMI, four new sub-Saharan African countries and one regional program in the Greater Mekong Sub-region of Southeast Asia were added in 2011. The contributions of PMI, together with those of other partners, have led to dramatic improvements in the coverage of malaria control interventions in PMI-supported countries, and all 15 original countries have documented substantial declines in all-cause mortality rates among children less than five years of age.

In 2015, PMI launched the next six-year strategy, setting forth a bold and ambitious goal with specific objectives. The PMI Strategy for 2015-2020 takes into account the progress over the past decade and the new challenges that have arisen. Malaria prevention and control remains a major U.S. foreign assistance objective and PMI's Strategy fully aligns with the U.S. Government's vision of ending preventable child and maternal deaths and ending extreme poverty. It is also in line with the goals articulated in the RBM Partnership's second global malaria action plan, *Action and Investment to defeat Malaria (AIM) 2016-2030: for a Malaria-free World* and WHO's updated *Global Technical Strategy 2016-2030*. Under the PMI Strategy 2015-2020, the U.S. Government's goal is to work with PMI-supported countries and partners to further reduce malaria deaths and substantially decrease malaria morbidity, towards the long-term goal of elimination.

Benin was selected as a PMI focus country in fiscal year (FY) 2007.

This FY 2016 Malaria Operational Plan (MOP) presents a detailed implementation plan for Benin, based on the PMI 2015-2020 strategy and the National Malaria Control Program (NMCP) strategy. It was developed in consultation with the NMCP and with the participation of national and international partners involved in malaria prevention and control in the country. The activities that PMI is proposing to support fit in well with the national malaria control strategy and plan and build on investments made by PMI and other partners to improve and expand malaria-related services, including the Global Fund to Fight AIDS, Tuberculosis, and Malaria (Global Fund) malaria grants. This document briefly reviews the current status of malaria control policies and interventions in Benin, describes progress to date, identifies challenges and unmet needs to achieving the targets of the NMCP and PMI, and provides a description of activities that are planned with FY 2016 funding.

2. Malaria situation in Benin

Benin is a West African coastal country that is bordered by Togo to the west, Nigeria to the east, and Burkina Faso and Niger to the north. The population from the 2013 national census was 9,983,884[1], representing a growth rate of 3.5% from the 2002 census. The infant mortality rate in Benin is 57 deaths per 1,000 live births. The maternal mortality rate is estimated to be 350 deaths per 100,000 live births and about 46% of people in Benin live in urban areas[2].

In health centers, more than 40% of malaria cases occur among children less than five years of age. According to the most recent Ministry of Health (MOH) national health statistics report from 2011, malaria is the leading cause of mortality among children under five and the leading cause of morbidity among adults in Benin. Trends for admissions and deaths due to malaria have steadily increased over the past four years. The World Health Organization (WHO) estimated that there were about 800 malaria hospital admissions and 23 malaria deaths per 100,000 population (all ages), in 2012[3]. The 2011-2012 Demographic and Health Survey (DHS) showed a parasitemia prevalence of 28% in children less than five years of age. Results from Benin's two most recent DHSs (2006 and 2011-2012), revealed a substantial decrease in the prevalence of anemia (malaria likely being a major cause) among children 6–59 months old, going from 78% in 2006 (25% mild, 46% moderate, and 8% severe) to 58% in 2011-2012 (26% mild, 29% moderate, and 3% severe).

Malaria is endemic to Benin, and while transmission is stable, it is influenced by several factors, including: vector species, geography, climate, and hydrography. The primary malaria vector in Benin is *Anopheles gambiae s.s.*, but secondary vectors are also important to transmission. For example, the widespread distribution and continuous breeding of *An. gambiae s.l.* in the south, and more seasonal breeding in the north, results in a nationwide endemic transmission pattern with three distinct regions. In the coastal region that has many lakes and lagoons, there are two vectors: *An. gambiae s.s.* (particularly *An. coluzzii:* the M form) and *An. melas* only in localities along Lake Oueme, Lake Aheme and Lake Porto-Novo. In the central region of the country, malaria is holoendemic, and *An. gambiae s.s. (An gambiae:* the S form and *An. coluzzii)* is the primary vector. In the northern-most region, malaria is seasonal, with a dry season (November to June) and a rainy season (July to October) during which malaria rates are highest. Recent entomological monitoring in 2012, and again in 2013[4], confirmed the presence of insecticide resistance to carbamates among mosquito vector populations on the eastern side of one department where IRS is planned.

---

[1] http://www.insae-bj.org/recensement-population.html accessed 12 March, 2015

[2] The World Statistics Pocketbook, 2014 edition (Series V, No. 38) Available on web at https://data.un.org/CountryProfile.aspx?crName=BENIN Accessed 09 March 2015.

[3] World Malaria Report 2013, page 106

[4] Africa Indoor Residual Spraying project. November 2012. *Semi-Annual Report, April-September 2012.* Bethesda, MD. Africa IRS project, Abt Associates Inc.

Figure 1. Benin: Malaria incidence in Benin, 2003-2013[*]

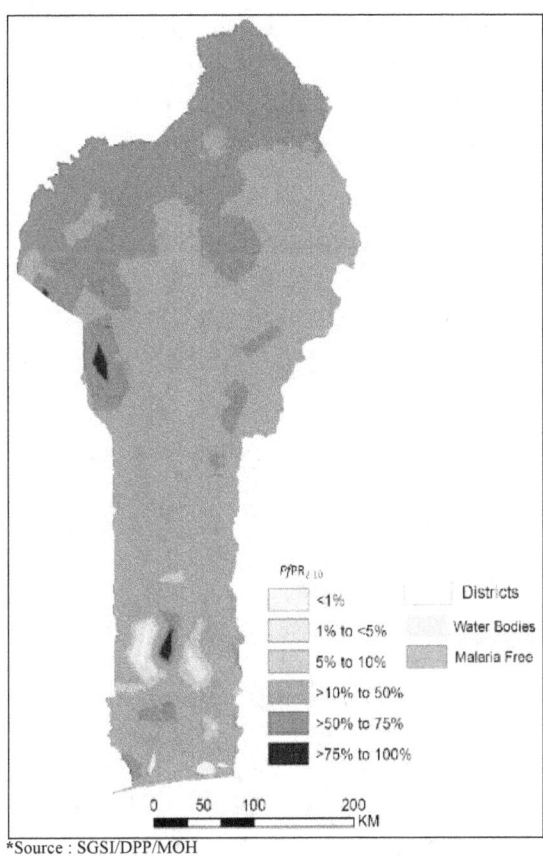

*Source : SGSI/DPP/MOH

3. Country health system delivery structure and Ministry of Health (MoH) organization

Administratively, Benin is divided into 12 departments, 77 communes, 546 *arrondissements*, and 3,747 villages. There are three metropolitan areas: Cotonou, Porto Novo, and Parakou. Benin's public health system fits within the administrative structure with a total of six health departments, which pair administrative departments, and 34 health zones, which pair an average of 2–3 communes with a population ranging from 84,000–492,000. There are three levels in Benin's pyramidal health system structure:

- Central: The MOH and its central Directorates, including the Directorate of Public Health to which the NMCP directly reports, along with one National Referral Hospital (*Centre National Hospitalier Universitaire*);
- Intermediate: The six Departmental Health Directorates, including an NMCP cell of dedicated staff and the corresponding six Departmental Referral Hospitals (*Centres Hospitaliers Départementaux*); and
- Peripheral: There are 34 health zones, including the following levels of clinical facilities in decreasing order of capacity: Zonal Hospitals (*Hôpitaux de Zone*); Commune Health Centers (*Centre de Santé de la Commune*), which includes inpatient services; accredited private health facilities; Community Health Centers (*Centres de Santé d'Arrondissement*), and village health units including Community Health Workers (CHWs).

In Benin, the private health sector is diverse and growing quickly. It is estimated that over half of the country's population receives health care services from the private sector, and a 2014 census of private sector clinics mapped 3,174 private facilities, 77% of which offer at least one maternal and child health service. Furthermore, 47% of the private sector clinics are unregistered, mainly due to an arduous accreditation process and low perceived benefits. Efforts are currently underway to reform the registration process in order to better align private providers' practices with national norms and standards. Other prominent types of private providers include traditional practitioners, licensed pharmacists, and informal drug vendors.

Nationwide, there are an estimated 12,500 CHWs, one-third of whom are female. National directives established primary education and residency in the community of service as requirements for all CHWs. These CHWs typically serve 30 households each and receive a performance-based stipend of $15-$25 per month administered through the local government, with financial support from donors, including UNICEF, USAID, and the Global Fund.

The directives also established two types of CHWs, CHWs who reside in communities less than five kilometers from a health facility and are responsible for health promotion only; and CHWs whose communities are more than five kilometers from a health facility, and who provide basic essential health services, including integrated community case management (iCCM). Since 2014, most CHWs providing basic health services have been trained on the use of RDTs and a national effort was undertaken to train CHWs on integrated case management for malaria, pneumonia, diarrhea, and malnutrition.

Following the recommendations of the 2013 Community Health Forum, a national community health policy was drafted and will be released during the year. The policy defines a local health system at the village and urban neighborhood level and promotes linking CHWs with public health facilities and local administration to establish a national community health program. The policy will also provide guidelines for roles and services provided, minimum qualifications required, and supervision, and performance incentives of community health actors. Finally, the policy will also develop new approaches to the unique access and service barriers of urban poor communities.

4. National malaria control strategy

Benin's National Strategic Plan (NSP) for 2011-2015 has been revised to extend through 2018. The revised plan takes into account the leading challenges sustained during the preceding five years, namely: adherence to case management guidelines and SP dosage for IPTp, regular and consistent use of ITNs, entomological monitoring for insecticide resistance, accurate and timely reporting on malaria morbidity and mortality, and appropriate supply chain management of antimalarials. The 2011-2018 NSP revised the long-term vision; it states, "By 2030, malaria will no longer be a public health problem in Benin". In order to realize this vision, the NMCP identified universal access to preventative interventions as well as proper treatment of malaria as main goals.

Primary objectives of the NSP include:

- Reducing by 75% the number of annual cases (from the number reported in 2000) and then maintaining that reduction.
- Reaching a national mortality rate of one death per 100,000 persons.
- Strengthening the management and coordination of the malaria program.

The NSP highlights continued implementation of key prevention strategies proven to be effective at the individual and community levels, e.g., sleeping under an ITN, IRS with long-lasting insecticides, as well as other anti-vector measures that minimize contact between humans and mosquitoes. Patients of all ages should receive a malaria diagnosis before receiving treatment, and treatment is free of charge for the most vulnerable populations: children under five years of age and pregnant women.

The NCMP implements the plan with a wide range of stakeholders including technical and financial partners. These partners participate in several technical malaria program working groups (monitoring and evaluation (M&E), behavior change communication (BCC), supply chain, entomology, and case management) and meet on a quarterly basis to review plans, activities, and make recommendations to the NMCP. Additionally, the NMCP uses monthly Roll Back Malaria (RBM) meetings as a platform for stakeholders to provide programmatic updates.

The NSP incorporates many elements of malaria control. The following are the key strategies outlined in the plan:

ITN:
- Pursuing universal access to long-lasting ITNs through continuous routine distribution to high-risk groups, combined with national distribution campaigns every three years.
- Strengthening design and piloting a school-based ITN distribution in 2017 (not currently funded).

IRS:
- Applying effective and environmentally sound practices using insecticide classes that are carefully selected and monitored entomologically.
- One IRS campaign conducted annually in one regional department of the country using an extended-release insecticide during high transmission season.

Anti larvicidal treatment:
- This activity is currently not funded but continues to remain in the NSP and targets both adult mosquitoes and larvae, when appropriate, with WHO Pesticide Evaluation Scheme (WHOPES)-approved insecticides.

MIP:
- Promoting free universal access of three doses of SP for pregnant women.
- Providing free bed nets to pregnant women at their first antenatal consultation.

Case management:
- Requiring diagnosis confirmed by microscopy or RDT for all suspected malaria cases prior to treatment with first-line ACTs, artemether-lumefantrine (AL) and artesunate-amodiaquine (AS/AQ), at all levels of care and in the community. The strategy is to provide free diagnosis and treatment of simple malaria for children less than five years of age and pregnant women and to refer clients with severe malaria for inpatient care.
- Improving the accuracy of diagnosis, availability of medicines, and accessibility to equipment to improve the implementation of malaria interventions.
- Expanding universal access to proper case management at the community level by increasing case management capacity and the coverage of community health workers in communities farther than five kilometers from a health facility.

Health system strengthening (HSS):

- This strategy focuses on the following building blocks of the health system: governance, human resource capacity, technical competence, managerial capacity, financial resource mobilization, supply chain management, public-private and international donor partnerships, as well as technical partnerships.

Surveillance and M&E:

- Optimizing NMCP management through systematic reviews and validation of M&E data collection activities, both during data analysis as well as during data collection in the field.
- Supporting the HMIS and periodic Malaria Indicator Surveys (MIS) to obtain accurate, timely, and useful data that is collected with efficiency and in harmony with other information systems.
- Reinforcing high quality RMIS data through production of quarterly bulletins and an annual publication. These publications are disseminated to health zones, health departments, and to technical and financial partners.
- Supporting surveillance and pharmacovigilance to monitor the sensitivity of malaria to recommended drugs, with appropriate investigation and reporting on any observed cases of resistance.

Operational research:

- The strategy proposes and promotes the importance of conducting operational research to measure impact of control and prevention activities, and to identify gaps and weaknesses in order to improve program implementation.
- Test promising innovations that could help accelerate the achievement of national targets in access, coverage, utilization, and impact.

BCC:

- Strategy is to use advocacy, behavior change communication, and social mobilization for the increased uptake of healthy behaviors related to the prevention of malaria.
- Increasing visibility through audiovisual applications, increased communication with partners, and updating website.

Private sector collaboration:

- Expand private sector collaboration to ensure that private health care providers align their diagnostic and therapeutic practices with national policies. This is strategically important due to the growing numbers of private clinics and practitioners who provide services to Benin's growing middle class.

Supply chain management:

- The NMCP closely coordinates with the Central Medical Stores (CAME) to ensure malaria medicines, products, and supplies are available. Additionally, they work with the National Directorate for Pharmacy and Laboratories to ensure regulatory functions and compliance on malaria-related issues.
- Strategy is to use different tools, including the Logistics Management and Information System (LMIS), end-use verification (EUV) survey, joint supervision visits, and weekly monitoring summaries, to give feedback and to improve supply chain management.

5. Updates in the strategy section

In February 2015, the Government of Benin (GOB) approved the updated NSP (2011–2018), which now aligns with the National Health and Development Plan (2008-2018). The objectives of the NSP remain unchanged; however, the update reflects greater engagement with the private sector in malaria control efforts and includes the recently approved IPTp guideline revision of three or more doses up until delivery and the treatment of severe malaria with injectable artesunate.

6. Integration, collaboration, and coordination

Benin's malaria stakeholders include local governments, civil society groups, the private sector, academia, and external donors. The MOH's NMCP, a unit of the National Directorate for Public Health *(Direction Nationale de la Santé Publique)*, is the government's recognized entity to ensure coordination and supervision of the country's malaria policy and program. Various civil society organizations act as implementing partners of the NMCP, especially at the community level and in remote areas where the MOH has little or no presence. Academia's role is to provide technical assistance, pre-service training, and continuing education. Representatives from the private sector, including private clinicians, individual service providers, commercial establishment owners, and vendors of goods and services also contribute to Benin's malaria program. PMI and the Global Fund are the principal donors to the NMCP. The Global Fund, complemented by PMI, provided most of the bed nets for mass distributions in 2011 and 2014. Both partners are also supporting community case management of malaria in selected health zones with promise for scale-up. The African Development Bank, the World Bank, and the Belgian Technical Cooperation have collectively provided district-focused results-based financing since 2012 with plans on a nationwide scale in 2015.

Relationships between the malaria stakeholders listed above are collegial and collaborative, and have been that way for several years. There continues to be adequate mechanisms in place to resolve issues of mutual concern and to encourage information sharing and harmonization of strategies and actions among Benin's malaria donors.

7. PMI goal, objectives, strategic areas, and key indicators

Under the PMI Strategy for 2015-2020, the U.S. Government's goal is to work with PMI-supported countries and partners to further reduce malaria deaths and substantially decrease malaria morbidity, towards the long-term goal of elimination. Building upon the progress to date in PMI-supported countries, PMI will work with NMCPs and partners to accomplish the following objectives by 2020:

1. Reduce malaria mortality by one-third from 2015 levels in PMI-supported countries, achieving a greater than 80% reduction from PMI's original 2000 baseline levels.

2. Reduce malaria morbidity in PMI-supported countries by 40% from 2015 levels.

3. Assist at least five PMI-supported countries to meet the World Health Organization's (WHO) criteria for national or sub-national pre-elimination.[5]

These objectives will be accomplished by emphasizing five core areas of strategic focus:
1. Achieving and sustaining scale of proven interventions
2. Adapting to changing epidemiology and incorporating new tools

---

[5] http://whqlibdoc.who.int/publications/2007/9789241596084_eng.pdf

3. Improving countries' capacity to collect and use information
4. Mitigating risk against the current malaria control gains
5. Building capacity and health systems towards full country ownership

To track progress toward achieving and sustaining scale of proven interventions (area of strategic focus #1), PMI will continue to track the key indicators recommended by the Roll Back Malaria Monitoring and Evaluation Reference Group (RBM MERG) as listed below:

- Proportion of households with at least one ITN
- Proportion of households with at least one ITN for every two people
- Proportion of children under five years old who slept under an ITN the previous night
- Proportion of pregnant women who slept under an ITN the previous night
- Proportion of households in targeted districts protected by IRS
- Proportion of children under five years old with fever in the last two weeks for whom advice or treatment was sought
- Proportion of children under five with fever in the last two weeks who had a finger or heel stick
- Proportion receiving an ACT among children under five years old with fever in the last two weeks who received any antimalarial drugs
- Proportion of women who received two or more doses of IPTp for malaria during ANC visits during their last pregnancy

8. Progress on coverage/impact indicators to date

National survey data show that progress is being been made for most malaria indicators in Benin, as measured by two DHSs (2006 and 2011-2012) and data from a 2014 MICS (conducted July – September), as outlined in Table A. It should be noted that the MICS was conducted prior to the national ITN campaign, which may explain the decrease in universal coverage and utilization among pregnant women. Estimates from the 2006 DHS, which was conducted from August–November 2006 (approximating the duration of the short rainy season), serve as the baseline indicators for Benin. The 2011-2012 DHS was conducted from December 2011-March 2012 (covering the dry season).

Household ownership of at least one ITN rose from 25% in 2006 to 80% in 2012, following mass distribution campaigns in 2007 and 2011. The 2014 MICS results report that 81% of households possessed at least one ITN. Utilization of ITNs by children under five rose from 20% in 2006 to 70% in 2012, and further, up to 73% in 2014. A concerning preliminary result from the recent 2014 MICS is a reported drop in the utilization of ITNs among pregnant from 75% in 2011-2012 DHS to 47% in 2014.

The proportion of pregnant women receiving at least two doses of IPTp with sulfadoxine-pyrimethamine (SP) from any source increased from 3% in 2006 to 23% in 2012. There is also notable progress in diagnosis and treatment. Comparing the proportion of children with fever who received prompt treatment with an ACT in the 2006 and 2012 surveys is difficult given the introduction of RDTs in 2011 and the diagnostic guidelines mandating that treatment be given only to patients with a positive test. The DHS 2011- 2012 reported that 17% of children under five who had a fever in the last two weeks received a diagnostic test, 7% received an ACT within 24 hours, and 38% received any type of antimalarial. The 2014 MICS reported similar indicators with 19% of children under five with a fever receiving a test, 13% receiving an ACT, and 26% receiving any type of antimalarial.

The proportion of women of childbearing age with any anemia (<11 g/dL) declined from 61% to 41% between 2006 and 2012. Similarly, prevalence of any anemia among children 6–59 months decreased from 78% in 2006 to 58% in 2012, and those with severe anemia (<8 g/dL) decreased from 16% to 7%. There is currently only one parasitemia data point for Benin, measured at 28% in children under five years of age during the 2011 – 2012 DHS.

Table A. Key Malaria Indicators in Benin

Indicator	2006 DHS	2011 - 2012 DHS	2014 MICS
% Households with at least one ITN	25	80	81
% Households with at least one ITN for every two people	NA	45	36
% Children under five who slept under an ITN the previous night	20	70	73
% Pregnant women who slept under an ITN the previous night	20	75	47
% Households in targeted districts protected by IRS	NA	80	83
% Children under five years old with fever in the last two weeks for whom advice or treatment was sought	37	39	44
% Children under five with fever in the last two weeks who had a finger or heel stick	NA	17	19
% Children receiving an ACT among children under five years old with fever in the last two weeks who received any antimalarial drugs	<1	7	13
% Women who received two or more doses of IPTp[1] during their last pregnancy in the last two years	3	23	38
% Women who received <u>at least three</u> doses of IPTp during their last pregnancy in the last two years	NA	NA	12

[1]In 2006, this measure was from any source: ANC or elsewhere. In 2012, this indicator only included SP/Fansidar sourced from ANC.

9. Other relevant evidence on progress

There are other indications that PMI is making progress in Benin. According to the DHS, from the pre-PMI period of 2001–2006 to the PMI scale-up period from 2006–2012, all-cause under-five mortality has decreased. There is a high degree of uncertainty around recent reductions in under-five mortality in Benin. The under-five mortality rates as reported by the DHS were 125 and 70 in 2006 and 2011-2012 respectively. This represents a decrease of 44%, but given the substantial differences observed in comparable periods for these data, there is reason to believe that the 2011-2012 figure may underestimate the true rate. The 2014 MICS reported an under-five mortality rate of 105, and has a comparable period much closer to that of the 2006 DHS. Thus, it is likely that the more modest reduction of 16% from 2006 to 2014 is a more likely representation of the reality in the population.

In September 2014, the country conducted its second mass bed net distribution campaign in hopes of achieving universal coverage. The first mass campaign in 2007 only targeted children under five years of age and pregnant women, while the 2011 mass distribution campaign targeted all ages. A rapid post-campaign evaluation conducted by the NMCP in November 2014, revealed that 85% of households surveyed had received at least one net during the 2014 campaign versus 86% in 2011. In addition, the results showed that, in 2014, 76% of households surveyed received at least one net for every two family members while in the 2011 campaign, only 56% had received at least one net for every two family members. The 2014 evaluation concluded that 93% of households possess at least one net– a finding consistent with the 94% possession of one or more nets following the 2011 campaign. Although preliminary, these numbers provide a trend in universal coverage with nets and raise some issues about net use that are discussed in the Insecticide-Treated Nets section of the MOP.

A baseline survey for a USAID-funded operational research project through the Child Survival and Health Grants Program (CSHGP) in the commune of Sémé-Kpodji (a mixed peri-urban and rural commune near Cotonou), reported a high demand for ITNs, where mothers confronted the survey team to demand that more ITNs be sent to the commune for vulnerable mothers and babies. The high demands reported in the baseline survey and the high levels of malaria knowledge among various groups as revealed in the 2011- 2012 DHS are likely due to behavior change campaigns supported by various malaria projects, including PMI. Beyond the PMI-funded BCC campaigns, the media in Benin have also been supportive in the dissemination of malaria information. There are weekly programs using various media channels. Over the years, radio outlets – whether religious, commercial or community – have complemented other media in disseminating information on malaria prevention. Benin's print media also contributed to informing the public on malaria prevention. PMI will continue to support the NMCP to improve knowledge of malaria among the general population and increase the use of preventive measures as well as case management tools available to reduce the malaria burden.

10. Challenges and opportunities

Challenges

Malaria is a major burden on the population's health and economy in Benin. The 2011-2012 DHS showed some progress in controlling the disease, but much more remains to be done before the goal of malaria no longer being a public health problem by 2030 is attained. Benin, like most developing countries, is plagued by the following challenges: (1) an acute health worker crisis, both in terms of quantity and the quality of services that health workers are trained to provide; (2) leadership and management skills, particularly for supervisory roles at the national, departmental, and district levels; (3) a national policy environment that has not allocated sufficient funds for health (e.g., only 6.8% of the 2014 national budget was allocated to health, well below the 2001 Abuja Declaration's recommended target of 15% for sub-Saharan African countries); (4) an HMIS that is still developing protocols and methodologies, particularly in routine monitoring and data quality; (5) a health infrastructure that has limited capacity to respond to or withstand sustained health emergencies; (6) incomplete implementation of national policies and treatment protocols.

Although the supply chain is showing improvement, additional efforts specific to strengthening data management and quantification of commodities are needed. While Benin has transitioned to quantification-based estimates using consumption data, critical obstacles remain in its pharmaceutical management system including: lack of formal agreements and poor communication between key supply chain partners, such as CAME and the NMCP; inadequate LMIS monitoring and supervision and tracking systems; and the need for software upgrades in Medistock. In addition, there is no formal system in place to track the distribution of free commodities, which contributes to poor data quality, shortages, stockouts, and overstocks.

Other challenges include a growing private sector that needs to be more engaged in malaria control and a growing urban population with little access to organized health services. Further, fake antimalarial drugs have an important presence in the markets of both the private and public sectors.

Although Benin is a small country, it is culturally diverse and linguistically complex, making communication of concepts and directives difficult, costly and time-consuming to implement. This is compounded by a large illiterate segment of the population: six out of ten adult women have never been to school. Implementing behavior change strategies at different levels requires effort and time in such a context.

Opportunities

Despite the above challenges, Benin has made substantial progress in the past few years. Changes in the HMIS data collection and the NMCP's management of IRS spraying in a district commune represent challenges that have become opportunities for the NMCP. There is a strong collaborative partnership between the MOH and donors. This creates a solid platform for continued scale-up of high impact interventions at the community level, which will contribute to the eventual elimination of malaria as a public health problem in Benin. This united effort led to the November 2013 Community Health Forum, a harmonized M&E plan for community health, the MOH/WHO/UNICEF/USAID partnership to scale-up integrated community case management, and the forthcoming Community Health Policy. Additionally, the recently revised NSP and new model for the Global Fund malaria proposal provide an opportunity to reframe priorities.

Decentralization of public sector health services is now being embraced by the MOH as a vehicle for accelerating coverage of malaria interventions and the expanding reach to other programs. This has started to generate opportunities for collaboration beyond the central level. At the health zone and department levels, donors have collaborative arrangements around local health issues that give communities a voice. Decentralization also expands the pool of human resources that could be mobilized for BCC activities and universal ITN distribution campaigns.

The increased involvement of the private sector constitutes a major opportunity to improve coverage of interventions in urban areas and reach the ever-growing middle class. With the existence of the *Coalition des Entreprises Béninoises et Associations Privées Contre le SIDA, la Tuberculose, et le Paludisme*, Benin hosted one of the first business coalitions formed to fight the three priority diseases in the Africa region, and they are a key player in promoting public-private partnerships against HIV, TB and malaria in the country. In 2014, a comprehensive national mapping of private sector clinics was completed and the MOH has accelerated the registration process for qualified, unlicensed clinics.

In 2010, performance-based financing (PBF), funded by the World Bank, the *Coopération Technique Belge*, the Global Fund, and the Global Alliance for Vaccines and Immunization, was introduced in 13 health zones. This approach will be scaled up to all 34 health zones in 2015. Several malaria services are compensated under this approach, including pregnant women receiving two or more doses of SP, pregnant women receiving an ITN, and pregnant women and children treated for malaria confirmed by microscopy or an RDT. In addition, health zone management teams are also compensated for supervision coverage based on the proportion of health facilities visited during the quarter. Community and for-profit private clinic components of PBF will also be rolled out in 2015.

Threats

Prolonged strikes in the public health sector limit the availability of services to the public. At the time of writing this MOP, health providers had been on strike for the past eight months, only providing services on a limited number of working days as well as emergency health services. During this period, it is very difficult to arrange site supervision or to receive timely routine reports.

Challenges of leadership, management, and governance capacity within the NMCP and other MOH units represent a constant threat to the effectiveness and sustainability of malaria interventions. This year, all the key positions in the NMCP were filled but high performing national program managers are quickly recruited by international agencies and consulting firms. Additionally, after a peak in 2010, the NMCP has seen a gradual reduction in external financial resources for malaria.

To ensure that activities undertaken by PMI continue beyond its period of support, the transfer of knowledge, capacity, and responsibilities to a strong NMCP and other government staff is vital. USAID/Benin is currently conducting a financial management risk assessment covering the NMCP's organizational, operational, and human resource capacity as well as a review of progress towards the recommendations from the 2009 institutional capacity assessment. This critical review is a key step towards direct government-to-government funding and capacity building as well as an important leveraging point for negotiating transformational conditions to address identified weaknesses.

Reforms of the Country Coordination Mechanism (CCM) had been very slow in Benin leading up to the installation of a new Board that was put into place in December 2014. Since this change, the CCM has met all the eligibility requirements to qualify for the Global Fund's new funding model and it successfully submitted all three concept notes, including malaria, in April 2015. The 2017 universal net distribution campaign is the main activity selected for this funding; however, costs of covering the entire population with free nets greatly exceeds the Global Fund's malaria funding available to Benin. As a result, PMI has had to redirect a quarter of its FY 2016 funding to procure one million ITNs to support the gap. This required funding cuts, particularly to the IRS intervention in Atacora Department, which will require prioritization of communes within the Department.

Aside from political and program issues, insecticide resistance threatens two of the four PMI interventions (ITNs and IRS). Resistance to pyrethroids used on ITNs, has shown to reduce the impact of IRS and ITNs[6]. Additionally, widespread vector resistance to two of the other three approved classes of IRS insecticides has emerged (see IRS entomology monitoring section). The presence of insecticide resistance to organochlorines, pyrethroids, and carbamates will be addressed through IRS insecticide rotation to organophosphates. Unfortunately, when organophosphate resistance appears (a likely outcome given its use in cotton cultivation), there is no current WHOPES-recommended alternative for further rotation.

---

[6]N'Guessan *et al.* Reduced efficacy of insecticide-treated nets and indoor residual spraying for malaria control in pyrethroid resistance area, Benin.*Emerg Infect Dis* 2007http://www.cdc.gov/EID/content/13/2/199.htm

III. OPERATIONAL PLAN

Over the past seven years, PMI has supported the GOB to implement its malaria control strategy, in partnerships with all national and international stakeholders, including local non-governmental organizations (NGOs) and the private sector. The progress described in this ninth Malaria Operational Plan (MOP) with key indicators represents major accomplishments documented by key surveys including the 2011-2012 DHS and the most recent 2014 MICS, using 2006 DHS as baseline. PMI supports Benin's malaria strategy, except the use of larviciding as a vector control tool.

1. Insecticide-treated nets

NMCP/PMI objectives

According to the NSP (2011-2018), the NMCP's objective is to achieve 100% coverage of the entire population, with all residents sleeping under an ITN by the end of 2018. The plan to achieve this coverage includes: (i) triennial mass distribution, providing free nets to all population groups (defined as one long-lasting insecticide-treated net for every two people) nationwide; and (ii) routine distribution of ITNs to pregnant women through ANC, children under five years of age through expanded program on immunization (EPI) clinic services, and to school children through primary and secondary schools. Social marketing is a complementary activity that contributes to the main distribution strategies.

Progress since PMI was launched

Since its launch in 2008, PMI has purchased and distributed approximately 4.9 million ITNs, of which 4 million were available for routine distribution and the remainder for social marketing and universal coverage campaigns. Approximately 5.3 million ITNs were distributed during the 2011 universal coverage campaign. These nets were provided primarily with Global Fund resources, with a portion obtained with World Bank Booster funds, and PMI contributing 150,000 nets. PMI also provided support for behavior change activities around the importance of using and maintaining ITNs as part of its broader BCC strategy, especially targeting the household level.

PMI has supported longitudinal studies on ITN durability, the results of which have now been combined with information from seven other PMI focus countries. The data show variability in life expectancy among different brands of ITNs; however, a decision on what the programmatic implication may be has yet to be determined. PMI/Benin also helped support a core-funded activity that intends to decrease malaria-related mortality by extending or preserving the operational life of ITNs.

The 2011-2012 DHS found that a majority of all households (80%) owned at least one ITN, and that 70% of children under five years of age and 75% of pregnant women reported that they had slept under an ITN the previous night. The 2014 MICS findings on ITN ownership and use the previous night by children under five years of age show slight improvements to 81%, and 73%, respectively. However, the MICS data suggests a drop in the proportion of pregnant women who reported sleeping under an ITN the previous night (47%). Still, overall, these data confirm significant progress in terms of ITN ownership and use since the 2006 baseline, when ownership and usage were both less than 25%.

Progress during the last 12-18 months

During the last 12 months, PMI procured, warehoused, and distributed 1,420,000 ITNs; the GOB allocated 680,000 nets for the 2014 universal net campaign, and 740,000 for routine services. On a pilot basis, PMI has distributed 1,100 nets in 2015 free of charge to pregnant women attending ANC through selected for-profit, private clinics. Currently, M&E tools to monitor facility distribution and social marketing include register books but facilities do not use these registers adequately to collect consumption data. PMI is advocating for greater use of these existing standardized pharmacy registers at public and participating private sector facilities for tracking consumption data that is entered into LMIS.

The second universal net campaign was launched in September 2014. In addition to net procurement, PMI provided technical assistance with the logistical and M&E coordination committees, while also providing monitoring and supervision in the field. During the past 12-18 months, PMI supported the training of both health facility and community health workers to communicate messages about continued use of ITNs. Further, PMI worked closely with the planning and organization of external technical assistance for the universal net campaign and routine distribution. Shortly after the national distribution, a rapid assessment was conducted, and the NMCP reported that 5,657,707 nets were distributed to 2,199,522 households. A more scientific and rigorous post-campaign evaluation, financially supported by Global Fund, is planned for early 2016. Pending Global Fund approval, the NMCP and Africare, as Principal Recipient, plan to conduct a Malaria Indicator Survey (MIS) in combination with this post-campaign evaluation.

Although the proportion of households in Benin who possess an ITN is relatively high (80%), universal coverage, (one bednet for every two persons) remains low. The 2011-2012 DHS measured universal access at 40%, and MICS 2014 preliminary data reports 36%. The next DHS is anticipated to be conducted in 2018. It will be important to carefully measure ITN utilization, correct placement, and overall access to ITNs during the evaluation. The NMCP and PMI are seeking ways to synergize existing activities that increase opportunities for messaging, and measurement of net access and appropriate net use.

Following the 2011 national universal net campaign, substantial gaps in ITN availability were reported due to the suspension of routine distribution of nets for several months, coverage gaps during the campaign, and shorter than expected net durability. Using some of the excess nets available from the distribution suspension, Peace Corps/Benin developed a temporary parallel system to provide nets to households to improve malaria prevention activities. In 2014, the Peace Corps conducted a needs assessment survey among 10,000 secondary school students across 75 communities where gaps were observed following the 2011 campaign. These communities were located across all 12 departments of Benin. About 80% of the participating students reported the need for at least one net. Survey results were shared with the NMCP who then authorized the distribution of 14,000 nets to identified households. As this distribution took place a few months prior to the 2014 universal campaign, Peace Corps collaborated with the health zones and local authorities to avoid duplication and unnecessary overlap. Using information from the NMCP's rapid post-campaign assessment and following confirmation of continued need and distribution gaps, future supplemental distribution will be implemented as needed.

Finally, PMI continues to support and strengthen entomological monitoring and evaluation of PMI vector control interventions in partnership with the *Centre de Recherche Entomologique de Cotonou*

(CREC). An OR activity (further detailed in the OR section) to track ITN loss is complete, with results already published.

Commodity gap analysis

Table B. ITN Gap Analysis

Calendar Year	2015	2016	2017
Total Targeted Population[1]	10,300,478	10,630,093	10,970,256
Continuous Distribution Needs			
Channel #1: ANC[2]	483,156	498,617	514,573
Channel #2: EPI (children < 5 years of age)[3]	349,432	360,614	372,154
Estimated Total Need for Continuous[4]	*832,588*	*859,231*	*886,727*
Universal Distribution Needs			
2017 universal distribution campaign[5]	--	--	6,094,587
Estimated Total Need for Campaigns	--	--	*6,094,587*
Total Calculated Need[6]: Routine and Campaign	**832,588**	**859,231**	**6,981,314**
Partner Contributions			
ITNs carried over from previous year	14,149	61,561	32,330
ITNs from MOH	80,000	100,000	150,000
ITNs planned with PMI funding	800,000	730,000	1,520,000[7]
ITNs from Global Fund New Funding Model	0	0	4,594,587
Total ITNs Available	**894,149**	**891,561**	**6,296,917**
Total ITN Surplus (Gap)	**61,561**	**32,330**	**(684,397)**

[1]The entire population is at risk.
[2]Pregnant women represent 5.2% of the population.
[3]Children under one year of age represent 4% of the population.
[4]Routine distribution needs assume a 100% ANC and vaccination attendance. Delivery through private accredited health facilities is permissible as long as PMI-funded commodities are provided free of charge to target population.
[5]Universal campaign needs are based on an estimated population of 10,970,256 at a ratio of 1.8 persons per net.
[6]Quantification estimates of need for the private sector are currently not available; however, USAID-supported ProFam clinics estimate a need of 10,450 ITNs for ANC clients in 2015 and 15,000 in 2016 and 2017.
[7]With FY 2016 funding, PMI plans to procure 1,000,000 ITNs for the universal campaign and 520,000 ITNs for routine distribution.

With carryover from previous years, we can assume that approximately 90% of the 2017 needs are covered. Based on the priority which the GOB will give to each distribution channel, ANC and EPI net needs through the public sector are entirely covered. A gap of 309,019 remains for the ANC private sector channel and a gap of 350,000 nets remains for the universal net distribution campaign; however, the campaign gap is likely to be filled by the Global Fund, either through reprogramming of under-expended lines in the new malaria agreement and/or the procurement of lower cost, standard sized nets which are slightly shorter than current national specifications.

Plans and justification

PMI will procure and ensure distribution of ITNs for the next universal net campaign, as well as for pregnant women through ANC services and for children receiving EPI services. PMI will work with the Global Fund and the NMCP to find ways to meet the remaining gap for the universal net campaign. PMI will continue to work with the NMCP and the accredited private sector to improve access to free ITNs distributed via routine ANC and EPI services as resources permit (see Case Management section for further information). In addition, PMI resources will be used for communication activities that support improved compliance for year-round ITN usage.

Proposed activities with FY 2016 funding: ($6,661,980)

1. *Procure and distribute ITNs for routine distribution:* PMI will procure and deliver approximately 520,000 long-lasting ITNs to health facilities for routine distribution through ANC and EPI services. Accredited, private sector facilities participating in routine distribution must provide PMI-funded ITNs for free to target populations. *($2,281,980)*

2. *Procure and distribute universal net campaign ITNs:* An estimated total of 6,094,587 nets are required to cover the Beninese population with an average of 1.8 persons per net for the 2017 universal net campaign. PMI will procure and distribute approximately 1,000,000 long-lasting ITNs for this campaign. *($4,380,000)*

2. Indoor Residual Spraying

NMCP/PMI objectives

The NSP (2011-2018) calls for universal access to IRS for all households in selected health zones to reduce mosquito populations and transmission as an integral part of the national vector control strategy. While the strategy calls for the selection of implementation zones based on entomological and epidemiological data, data quality limitations make such selection challenging. The 2012-2015 national management plan for malaria vector resistance to insecticides follows WHO recommendations for rotation of insecticides and mosaic spraying with entomological surveillance to monitor vector sensitivity to insecticides.

CREC manages 11 entomological surveillance sites nationwide, including four sites in the current sprayed areas in Atacora Department (sites: Natitingou, Tanguieta, Kouande, and Pehunco) and a control site in Copargo in Donga Department. The remaining six sites are based in Adjohoun in Ouémé Department; Pobe in Plateau Department; Ouidah in Atlantique Department; Dassa in Collines Department; Parakou in Borgou Department, and Kandi in Alibori Department. These surveillance sites provide routine data on mosquito population dynamics and insecticide resistance in Benin. The level of vector resistance is mapped and regularly documented with the support of national research institutions and universities. The NMCP collaborates with the national research centers, notably CREC, to monitor resistance to inform insecticide selection. Coordination across all ministries implicated in vector control remains a priority area for improvement in the NSP.

PMI is the sole funder of IRS activities in Benin and efforts to mobilize additional funding resources have been thus far unsuccessful. The combination of growing insecticide resistance, increased cost of new insecticides, and static funding is a critical challenge stated in the NSP.

Progress since PMI was launched

Spraying began in 2008 in the Ouémé Department located in the south. However, the malaria transmission season in that region outlasted the duration of the IRS insecticidal effect. Therefore, after three rounds of spraying in Ouémé, IRS operations moved to the northern department of Atacora, where the transmission season is shorter. Entomological monitoring in 2014[7] confirmed continued presence of vector-insecticide resistance to pyrethroid- and carbamate-class insecticides in malaria vector populations from the eastern side of Atacora (Table C). Future IRS will continue to rely on organophosphate-class insecticides.

Table C. Insecticide susceptibility[1] of *An. gambiae s.l.*populations in IRS districts, 2014: % mortality[1]

Location	Insecticide Class[2]	Number Tested	Average Mortality (%)	Susceptible (S) /Resistant (R)
Tanguieta	Pyrethroid (PY) Delthamethrin SC-PE	NA[3]	NA	R
	Carbamates (CA) Bendiocarb WP (Ficam)	98	79	R
	Organophosphates (OP) Pirimiphos methyl WP and EC Pirimiphos methyl CS (Actellic 300 CS)	106	100	S
Pehunco	Pyrethroid (PY)	NA[3]	NA	R
	Carbamates (CA) Bendiocarb WP (Ficam)	116	80	R
	Organophosphates (OP) Pirimiphos methyl WP and EC Pirimiphos methyl CS (Actellic 300 CS)	103	99	S

[1]WHO vector-insecticide susceptibility test. When mosquito mortality falls below 80%, the general recommendation has been to rotate away from that insecticide class.
[2]OP-organophosphate class insecticide, CA-carbamate class insecticide, PY-pyrethroid class insecticides
[3]Number tested and % mortality for pyrethroids not available in the 2014 CREC entomologic report

The 2015 round of IRS will mark the fifth year of spraying in Atacora. Table D summarizes PMI's annual IRS activities. Recent entomologic surveillance now shows that transmission in Atacora lasts more than four months. It is permanent, but high, between June and November (six months). The residual effect of previously used insecticides lasts up to four months. PMI expects that the longer-lasting pirimiphos methyl formulation used this year will adequately cover the transmission season.

---

[7]Centre de Recherche Entomologique de Cotonou. 2014. Monitoring-Evaluation of the efficacy of the fourth round of Indoor Residual Spraying (IRS) in Atacora, using perimiphos methyl CS formulation and mapping of malaria transmission and insecticide resistance in sentinel sites, Benin. CREC/USAID/PNLP/Report Doc Dec 2014.

Table D: PMI-supported IRS activities (2008 –2017)

Year	Number of Communes Sprayed	Department	Insecticide Used	Number of Structures Sprayed	Coverage Rate	Population Protected
2008	9	Ouémé	Carbamate	142,813	94%	521,698
2009	9	Ouémé	Carbamate	156,223	99%	512,491
2010	9	Ouémé	Carbamate	166,910	99%	636,448
2010	9	Ouémé	Carbamate	200,036	99%	623,904
2011	7	Atacora	Carbamate	145,247	96%	426,232
2012	9	Atacora	Carbamate	210,380	94%	652,777
2013	9	Atacora	Organophosphate(EC) (5 communes) Carbamate (4 communes)	228,951	95%	694,729
2014	9	Atacora	Organophosphate (EC,CS)	254,072	95%	789,883
2015	9	Atacora	Organophosphate (CS)	252,706	94%	802,597
2016	9	Atacora	Organophosphate	~250,000	TBD	~800,000
2017	TBD	Atacora	Organophosphate	TBD	TBD	TBD

PMI supports in-country IRS capacity building, including work, study, and research opportunities at CREC for the National University of Abomey – Calavi graduate students. The scaling up of CREC's entomology unit, organized to implement the PMI-supported entomology/IRS M&E work plan, has provided field research opportunities to many qualified students. This relationship has given rise to an estimated 34 graduate-level scientists with strong malaria control experience. There are 26 graduates with or pursuing masters' degrees and six doctoral-level degrees[8] (including two recent PhD graduates among leadership staff from NMCP) with malaria control experience, including direct experience in IRS. These experts have published 26 articles in referred journals.[9] In addition, students and persons trained by CREC have graduated to assume visible and productive roles in ongoing malaria prevention and control efforts in Benin and in multiple sectors of the work force.

Progress during the last 12-18 months

The 2014 IRS campaign in Atacora supported the spraying of approximately 250,000 structures protecting 790,000 persons. Building on experience gained through a 2014 WHO mentoring grant award[10] to support NMCP/IRS capacity building, the NMCP managed IRS in three of the nine communes targeted by IRS. In addition to day-to-day partnering between the NMCP and PMI's implementing partner, PMI supports capacity building in IRS operations including micro-planning, supervision and post-IRS evaluation. The resulting IRS network provided for greater NMCP confidence,

---

[8]Centre for Entomologic Research of Cotonou (CREC). Contribution of PMI to strengthening the research and training capacity of CREC. Ministry of Health, Benin report 2014.

[9]Ministry of Health 2014. CREC's scientific publications supported by PMI/USAID (2010-2014). Center for Entomologic Research (CREC)

[10] TDR Training and fellowship opportunities: http://www.who.int/tdr/grants/empowerment/en/index.html. Short-term grant proposal for knowledge management to help improve malaria control in Benin."Strengthening the National Malaria Control Program (PNLP), Ministry of Health (MOH), Bénin capacity to conduct indoor residual sprayihg (IRS) for malaria control.Awarded January, 2014.

comprehensive on-the-job training, a vision for independent NMCP management of IRS, and a strong technical support structure during the spray season. The NMCP successfully managed IRS operations in the commune of Tanguieta in 2014; similar results were achieved in the larger, three commune area, managed by the NMCP in 2015.

Despite the high sprayed structure coverage rate and quality entomological surveillance data, there is concern about the future of IRS in Benin. The 2017 IRS campaign will suffer a decline in resources due to the need for additional funding to support the universal ITN campaign. While only a temporary reduction, given existing ento- and epidemiological data limitations, determining which geographic areas will be challenging. Faced with this situation, PMI is working with the MOH to convene a high-level national consultation this year, bringing together national stakeholders, to reassess the current direction and establish a short, medium, and long-term plan for IRS in Benin for greater efficiency and maximized public health benefit. A road map will determine how best to use the 2017 resources to continue to build local capacity among government partners (e.g. the NMCP and CREC), support comprehensive monitoring of insecticide resistance to ensure efficacy of insecticide selection, and strengthen epidemiological data quality for decision-making.

Plans and justification

During 2017, IRS activities will be marked by a temporary reduction in funding, resulting in a decline in IRS coverage. Methods to determine which communes to select for spraying are still under discussion. PMI will continue to support entomological monitoring (vector sporozoite infection rate, vector-pyrethroid resistance levels) and ITN durability monitoring (coverage, fabric integrity, bio-efficacy) at existing national entomological surveillance sites.

Proposed activities with FY 2016 funding: ($2,295,000)

1. *IRS implementation and management:* PMI plans to support one round of spray operations, using a long-lasting organophosphate insecticide formulation, to cover structures in prioritized communes of the Atacora Department. Support includes the cost of equipment and insecticide procurement, planning, community mobilization, spraying implementation, and environmental compliance. Within this activity, PMI will continue to build IRS capacity among Beninese counterparts through mentoring of graduate students and graduates. *($2,100,000)*

2. *Entomological monitoring:* PMI will support monthly cone test bioassay entomological monitoring at all 11 sentinel sites nationwide to measure mosquito population dynamics for potential future IRS intervention. In Atacora, PMI will support insecticide resistance monitoring in four sites (Natitingou, Tanguieta, Kouande, and Pehunco). At these sites, monitoring will assess vector kill rates on IRS structures, and ongoing insecticide efficiency, including longevity of the insecticide on the walls. Insecticide resistance monitoring will also be measured in a control site in Copargo. *($160,000)*

3. *Vector control supplies:* Equipment and replacement supplies for traps, sprays, and landing catches, storage of specimens, and related laboratory supplies will be procured by PMI and sent to Benin for entomological monitoring activities. *($6,000)*

4. *Technical assistance:* An entomologist from CDC will provide a total of two technical assistance visits. One TDY will provide continued technical assistance through supervision and

training related to entomology/IRS M&E, specifically: strategic planning with CREC and NMCP around issues related to the application of vector-insecticide resistance results to IRS plans; programmatic planning with CREC/NMCP following results from the PMI/Benin ITN tracking study; and to conduct additional training in expanded measurement of ITN surface insecticide levels by means of CDC colorimetric fast test methods. The second TDY is requested to further develop strategic plans for the national IRS partnership. *($29,000)*

3. Malaria in pregnancy

NMCP/PMI objectives

The NSP (2011-2018) for MIP, which was developed by the NMCP in collaboration with the National Directorate for Maternal and Child Health (DSME), has four components: (i) free distribution of SP for the intermittent preventive treatment for pregnant women (IPTp); (ii) free distribution of ITNs during first contact with ANC; (iii) provision of iron/folate (200mg dose of iron and 5mg dose of folate) , and; (iv) administration of oral quinine during the first trimester and ACTs in the second and third trimesters for treatment of uncomplicated malaria, and use of quinine during all trimesters for treatment of severe malaria. Pregnant women who are HIV-positive are treated following standard WHO guidelines.

The NMCP target is that by the end of 2018, 100% of pregnant women sleep under an ITN and will have received a full course of IPTp (as per the national guidelines). In January 2015, the national IPTp guidelines were aligned with the WHO standard to provide monthly observed SP/Fansidar® treatments starting early in the second trimester of pregnancy up to the time of delivery. While there is a plan to update the routine information system this year to account for the three or more doses, currently IPTp2 is still reported as a performance measure.

Progress since PMI was launched

Since 2008, PMI procured approximately 6 million SP treatments for IPTp, trained 1,610 public and 134 private health workers on MIP, and reached more than 3.5 million people with communication messages promoting IPTp uptake and nightly use of ITNs for the prevention of malaria in pregnancy.

Routine ANC distribution of ITNs is functioning well and PMI to date has been able to provide all routine nets for pregnant women in Benin since the program started in 2008. The 2011-2012 DHS showed a high rate of ITN use among pregnant women (75%), compared with 20% in 2006. However, the MICS data suggests a drop in the proportion of pregnant women who reported sleeping under an ITN the previous night (47%). Potential causes of this decline need to be investigated as there has been change in ITN availability over the past 12-18 months.

Results from the 2011-2012 DHS also show that 86% of pregnant women make at least one ANC visit, 81% of pregnant women make two or more ANC visits, and 58% of pregnant women make four or more ANC visits. Attendance rates are higher in urban areas than in rural areas (91% versus 82%); however, there is only a marginal difference between rates of IPTp2 coverage between urban and rural areas (24% versus 22%, respectively). While IPTp2 coverage has improved from 3% to 25% according to the 2006 and 2011-2012 DHS, and reached 43% according to the 2014 national RMIS reports, it still falls short of the PMI and NMCP targets of 85% and 100% respectively. Data from the 2014 MICS indicates that 12% of pregnant women received three or more doses (regrettably, it did not report on two or more doses). While ANC visits are high, a challenge to achieving universal coverage of IPTp3 or more treatments will be to ensure delivery of correct IPTp among private sector providers who provide nearly half of all ANC consultations in Benin.

The 2012 barrier assessment to IPTp in two health zones in Benin conducted by PMI continues to inform the IPTp improvement approach, which focuses on improving availability of SP at the ANC service delivery point, addressing perceived negative consequences of taking SP during pregnancy by both health workers and mothers, and improving quality of reception and organization of ANC consultations. Several social barriers were also identified and are reported in the BCC section of this document. ANC kits are still promoted in the public health clinics at first ANC visits. The cost remains 500 CFA (about one dollar) to recover costs to the health facility for the mebendazole and iron-folate. The PMI-supported formative research did not reveal this cost as one of the major barriers to IPTp uptake.

Progress during the last 12-18 months

During the last 12 months, PMI procured 1,517,536 treatments of SP, which covers almost 100% of the nationwide need. Of the 720,000 ITNs that PMI procured and distributed for routine service delivery, over 470,000 were targeted for ANC. A total of 740,000 ITNs have been ordered for 2015, and 488,000 of these will be made available for pregnant women through distribution at ANC clinics.

In 2014, PMI conducted refresher training of 543 public health workers and an initial training of 156 private health workers on IPTp. In total, 608 professionals were trained on interpersonal communication. PMI has also supported the MOH to supervise health workers, improve quality of services, strengthen logistics management for malaria in pregnancy commodities, improve BCC activities promoting ANC attendance, procure approximately one million treatments of SP, and educate pregnant women and communities on the risks of malaria in pregnancy and the benefits of IPTp.

In 2013-2014, PMI trained 409 midwives and 512 nurses on the MIP guidelines which were updated to align with the new WHO recommendations for three or more treatments. It is estimated that most professional antenatal care providers have been trained. However, in several sites, less qualified staff provide antenatal care and should also be considered for future training opportunities. Further, in 2014, the GOB recruited 1,134 additional providers and another 7,000 new recruits are anticipated over the next two years as the country retires a large cohort of health workers. PMI is supporting the NMCP to complete a training situation analysis to more definitely express the gap for both professional and non-professional staff. It will be important to track and train new recruits as well as ensure that pre-service training is based on the latest guidelines.

The RMIS indicates that some health zones are achieving IPTp2 coverage above 50%. PMI is preparing a best practices event this year to document and disseminate promising approaches for replication.

Commodity gap analysis

While the government procured some 200,000 treatments in 2014, there were no known commitments beyond PMI for purchasing SP for the public and private sectors in Benin.

Table E. SP Gap Analysis for Malaria in Pregnancy (2015-2017)

Calendar Year	2015	2016	2017
Total Population	10,300,478	10,630,093	10,970,256
SP Needs			
Total number of pregnant women attending ANC	488,243	503,866	519,990
Total SP Need (in treatments [3 pills])[1]	**1,464,729**	**1,511,598**	**1,559,970**
Consumption data estimate	**2,132,280**	**2,558,736**	**3,019,308**
Partner Contributions			
SP carried over (deficit) from previous year	n/a	n/a	n/a
SP from MOH	0	0	0
SP from Global Fund	0	0	0
SP from Other Donors	0	0	0
SP planned with PMI funding	1,050,000	1,072,222	1,650,000
Total SP Available	**1,050,000**	**1,072,222**	**1,650,000**

[1]SP need in treatments comes from quantification 2014 based on consumption data and not number of pregnant women attending ANC multiplied by three.

[2]The total SP surplus/gap estimate is based on demographic data. While the NMCP quantification technical working group prefers to use consumption data, PMI supports a review and adjustment of the parameters used in its first quantification for SP conducted in 2014 rather than reversion to the use of demographic or epidemiological data estimates.

Plans and justification

PMI will continue to support activities aimed at enhancing the provision of effective MIP services in both public and accredited private health facilities in Benin. Further, the program will promote MIP intervention uptake at the community level. To that end, PMI will procure enough SP treatments to cover nationwide need. SP will be delivered through both the public and participating accredited private sector health clinics (faith-based, non-profit, and for-profit), free of charge to pregnant women. PMI will support laboratory diagnosis and appropriate treatment of malaria to reinforce the implementation of MIP services, including supervision of IPTp service delivery along with other aspects of effective case management, and promotion of ITN use.

Proposed activities with FY 2015 funding: ($466,000)

1. *Procure SP.* PMI will procure 1,650,000 SP treatments to contribute to the national supply for both public and private facilities. *($297,000)*

2. *Support for supervision and refresher training in IPTp:* PMI will reinforce existing results-based financing in place nationwide for ITNs and SP for pregnant women. Quality improvement activities will be supported that facilitate provider-initiated SP monthly to all pregnant women

starting early in the second trimester and up to delivery, closing the gap between SP1 and SP3+, through better record keeping, coaching, and supervision. PMI will provide support for integrated on-site supervision of health workers and refresher training to ensure correct practices regarding IPTp uptake and promotion of the prevention of malaria in pregnancy. *($169,000)*

4. Case management

a. Diagnosis and Treatment

NMCP/PMI objectives

The NSP (2011-2018) sets the following objectives:

- 100% of all suspected malaria cases in public and accredited private health facilities as well as community-level are tested.
- 100% of all confirmed malaria cases in public and accredited private health facilities as well as community-level are treated correctly (as per national guidelines).
- 100% of severe malaria cases in public and accredited private health facilities are managed correctly (as per national guidelines).

The national malaria case management guidelines follow WHO guidelines and standards. The first-line treatment drug for uncomplicated malaria is artemether-lumefantine (AL). The two exceptions to this are infants under six months of age and pregnant women in their first trimester, where the recommended treatment is artesunate-amodiaquine (AS/AQ) and quinine, respectively. All severe cases of malaria should be treated with injectable artesunate or quinine. Injectable artesunate is available at CAME and plans are in place to promote it as the first-line treatment for severe malaria across all hospitals nationwide with the upcoming release of the updated case management guidelines. Severe cases identified in peripheral sites should be referred to a facility with inpatient capacity and it is recommended that injectable artesunate or artesunate suppositories be given for pre-referral treatment. AS/AQ, the first-line malaria treatment for children under six months of age, is procured directly by the GOB.

The NMCP is preparing a national dissemination of the revised guidelines at the intermediary and peripheral levels in 2015 to reinforce the clinical importance of switching to injectable artesunate as the first-line treatment for severe malaria.

Since 2011, Benin launched a free malaria treatment policy for children under five years of age and pregnant women. This free treatment policy has been implemented at the community level utilizing CHWs, trained in integrated community case management (iCCM) including RDT use, as well as in public clinics and hospitals. Implementation of the free treatment policy in the formal private sector has proven extremely challenging given the for-profit nature of their business. Furthermore, in 2014, public facilities phased into a PBF mechanism that renumerates facilities and providers for treatment of confirmed malaria cases. Facilities complain of limited funds for replenishing ACT supplies due to the slow reimbursement process. Introduction of PBF in the private sector as well as at the CHW level is on schedule to start in 2015.

The current malaria policy promotes the use of RDTs throughout the health system but access to RDTs and microscopy continues to be a challenge, particularly at the peripheral level. In 2014, RMIS data with 83% of all health facilities reporting show that 84% of all reported malaria cases were tested by either microscopy or RDT. However, the DHS 2011-2012 and the 2014 MICS report respectively that only 17% and 19% of children under five years of age with fever received a diagnostic test for malaria.

In 2013, the NMCP began an effort to improve peripheral level malaria diagnosis by increasing the available stock of RDTs as well as the number of CHWs trained in RDT use. To date, roughly 9,000 of the 12,500 CHWs have been trained in RDT use, including 1,500 in zones supported by PMI. Training on RDTs to the remaining CHWs is covered with current Global Fund support. However, at the national level, there is still a need to continue retraining CHWs and health facility workers to perform RDTs.

Progress since PMI was launched

Since 2008, PMI has worked to build laboratory diagnostic capacity through training, supervision, and purchasing laboratory equipment and supplies. The need for microscopes is defined by the NMCP as a minimum of two microscopes for every departmental and health zone hospital, and one microscope for every commune health center. A 2013 nationally representative health facility survey of 60 public and private health centers found that only 55% of facilities had the capacity to perform either microscopy or RDTs, which largely reflects the capacity of public non-hospital facilities to perform malaria diagnostics at 54%. To date, PMI has purchased 80 microscopes, but the NMCP estimates a need of 40 additional microscopes to cover departmental hospitals, health zones, and communal health centers through 2015. In order to help fill this gap, PMI plans to purchase another 15 microscopes in 2015. PMI does not have plans to support development of a slide bank or EQA program.

PMI supports a comprehensive diagnostics strengthening program that involves training clinicians and laboratory technicians, implementation of quality assurance and control systems, and improved supervision to ensure adherence to clinical guidelines. In February 2011, the NMCP updated Benin's malaria case management guidelines to recommend universal diagnostic testing for malaria. Following this new policy, PMI supported training, supervision, and assistance to increase clinical staff's awareness and implementation of the new national policy and guidelines. At health facilities, more than 2,500 health workers were trained and certified in malaria laboratory diagnostics (either RDTs or microscopy). To monitor adherence to malaria diagnosis practices, PMI has supported two nationally representative health facility surveys (2009 and 2013) and continues to collect routine surveillance data on key malaria indicators. Furthermore, PMI has supported improvements to the RMIS system that was established in 2011.

Approximately 6.8 million ACT treatments have been procured from 2008 to 2014. Most government health staff and CHWs have been trained to diagnose and treat malaria as recommended according to the 2011 guidelines. PMI has also supported refresher trainings on the management of uncomplicated malaria, including confirmatory testing using RDTs, and supportive supervision of 1,500 health facility workers in integrated management of childhood illness (IMCI) across all 34 health zones nationwide.

Since 2009, PMI has supported CHWs to provide quality integrated community case management (iCCM) of malaria, diarrhea, acute respiratory infections and screening for acute malnutrition. Through this work, PMI has assisted in the development of national training curricula, supervision standards, as well as community monitoring and evaluation systems.

USAID/Benin supports the MOH effort to accelerate the scale-up iCCM nationwide. USAID/Benin's strategy is to contribute to national scale-up of iCCM by doubling its coverage from five to ten health zones by 2015. The expansion zones were selected in collaboration with the DSME, and the NMCP based on the need to sustain existing USAID/Benin-supported CHW networks and to improve access to care for underserved populations.

Given its importance in health service delivery to nearly half of the population, PMI supports improving malaria case management at accredited private health facilities in Benin. In 2013, USAID/Benin mapped over 3,000 private clinics, many of which are not yet registered with the Ministry of Health. Since 2014, PMI has supported the fast tracking of 179 for-profit and non-profit private clinics' registration requests of which 80 have been approved and 99 are pending. Furthermore, PMI has trained 289 providers from 22 for-profit and non-profit private clinics in malaria case management. Important progress has been made in RMIS reporting by the registered private clinics. Despite these gains, much more work needs to be done to strengthen regulations, improve quality of data reporting, and improve private sector access to malaria commodities (RDTs, ACTs, SP, ITNs) to improve access to the population. While accredited private health facilities procure essential health commodities from CAME, national program commodities including malaria are restricted to the public sector.

PMI developed four training modules including a training manual, participating nurse's and doctor's manuals, and an orientation manual for pharmacists. In spite of the amount of training and supervision supported to date by PMI and other partners, health worker performance still needs improvement. Preliminary results of the 2013 PMI-supported national survey of 60 public and private sector outpatient health facilities found that 96% health workers had received some type of training in ACT use, but only 56% had at least one supervision visit in the past six months and 48% had any type of ACT in stock the day of the survey. Furthermore, not all patients with suspected malaria were tested, and patients with severe malaria often did not receive pre-referral treatment according to national guidelines. However, early results from this same survey suggest that nearly all patients (87%) who tested positive were given antimalarials.

Progress during the last 12-18 months

During the last 12 months, PMI has provided 2 million RDTs and basic materials for the maintenance and repair of microscopes. PMI procured 2,032,170 ACTs to help meet the national gap and there was no central level stockout. PMI also supported the NMCP to develop guidelines for a shared procurement planning approach for malaria commodities provided by the GOB, the Global Fund, PMI, UNICEF, the World Bank, and other sources. This approach aims to improve product availability for the national program and is scheduled for validation and implementation in 2015.

Over the past year, PMI has supported efforts to improve facility health workers' adherence to national malaria case management guidelines that recommend laboratory confirmation of all suspected malaria cases. End-use verification (EUV) surveys conducted in three departments in 2014 indicated that 90-95% of children less than five years of age that presented with fever had correctly received ACTs and that administration of ACTs to non-confirmed cases had decreased to less than 8%.

PMI supported a malaria collaborative quality improvement effort with the Abomey-Calavi/Sô-Ava health zone to improve the management of uncomplicated malaria cases in 17 public health facilities. Peer validated data has shown improvements; for example, the proportion of children under five years of age with confirmed malaria who were correctly treated with an ACT increased from 33% to 92% (n=8,697) from January 2013 to June 2014. It is noted that these results are better than the 80% of all confirmed malaria cases treated with any antimalarial. Similar improvements were reported among clients over five years of age, with proportions increasing from 14% to 98% during the same period (n=19,641). Monthly data quality verification by external coaches, team problem solving, sharing results, and promoting a spirit of competition among health facility teams, together with regular follow-up by the health zone management team are important factors that contributed to this improvement.

According to recent annual reporting, during the past year, semi-annual or quarterly supervision visits to maintain and improve quality microscopy and RDT diagnoses were conducted in 68 facilities. An annual report of last year's supervision of health facilities' data showed that 84% of the 68 health facilities included in the latest round of outreach training support and supervision (OTSS) visits were capable of performing biological diagnosis of malaria (either microscopy or RDT).

In the past 12 months, PMI supported the expansion of the Emergency Triage Assessment and Treatment (ETAT) approach from 12 to 25 hospitals, along with the installation of 12 oxygen concentrators. The ETAT program aims to improve case management for severe malaria, and performance against national standards and case fatality rates are monitored at each site monthly. From January 2013 to October 2014, phase 1 ETAT hospitals showed improved case management compliance with ETAT norms from 50% to 87% and a decrease in the severe malaria case fatality rate from 6 to 3.4.

To transfer resources to the health zones for malaria performance improvement (through supervision, quality assurance, and training), PMI's implementing partner completed memorandums of understanding to reimburse malaria supervision activities for all 34 health zones nationwide. This approach was successful in engaging all six health departments to review implementation fidelity; however, performance improvement was not well measured and some zones have been reluctant to embrace and implement their action plans and reimbursement claims. In 2014, PMI supported the supervision of 561 health facilities in 27 zones.

In 2014, PMI facilitated the training of 289 private sector health workers on malaria diagnostics and case management while also facilitating the registration of 80 private clinics. Another 99 private health facilities have been identified for support to complete their registration with the MOH. PMI is supporting a pilot to facilitate access to malaria commodities to 57 ProFam clinics, a USAID-supported network of accredited, private, for-profit health facilities established since 2006. The approach for facilitating access to commodities is under national discussion and two options are being studied: a) allow access to malaria commodities through CAME to providers offering free malaria treatment to children under five years of age and pregnant women; b) implement social marketing of low cost, quality controlled RDTs, ACTs, SP, and ITNs. Hybrids of these concepts are also under consideration. As per PMI policy, PMI-funded commodities can only be distributed free of charge to clients; therefore, in the event that the latter option is selected, an alternative source for commodities will need to be identified.

In collaboration with UNICEF and the Global Fund, PMI supported a joint implementation plan to train and equip more than 1,500 CHWs in iCCM, including certified training in the use of RDTs, in five high priority health zones in northern Benin. PMI supported supervision of CHWs and reporting of iCCM data. In 2014, 17,375 children under five years of age were tested with RDTs and 16,407 malaria cases were correctly treated with ACTs.

In October 2014, USAID/Benin completed the transition to direct funding for two NGOs with significant iCCM experience. These local NGOs will support the MOH to operationalize the package of high impact interventions (PIHI), including iCCM in two health zones each. The third NGO, new to iCCM, has demonstrated capacity in community and reproductive health and operates in a new PMI-supported health zone. Capacity building and technical assistance, including bi-monthly supervision and data quality validation, is coordinated by USAID/Benin with its PMI-funded partner.

However, some challenges to achieving 100% testing of suspect cases and 100% treatment of confirmed cases remain, including stockouts at point of service delivery, engagement with the private sector to adhere to national case management guidelines, and evidence that some workers at health facilities do not fully embrace RDTs, but revert to microscopy as the single diagnostic option. Additionally, the parallel use of different types of RDTs with differing operating procedures is a barrier to systematic messages and evaluations of performance. Finally, better record keeping of RDT and ACT use, needs and consumption, from LMIS and HMIS along with continued alignment of the private sector with national guidelines are crucial to increasing testing of suspected malaria cases. Furthermore, a new cohort of public health workers entered the system in 2014 and requires malaria-specific training. PMI is working with the NMCP to plan trainings for these new recruits as well as develop the malaria training strategy, which will include a greater focus on pre-service training.

Commodity gap analysis

a. RDTs

The estimated need for RDTs in 2017 is 11,726,298. This projection includes the private sector, public health facilities, and community-level needs. With FY 2016 funding, PMI will purchase 1.8 million RDTs to cover some of the country's gap. In 2015, existing microscopy capacity will be reinforced in hospitals and larger health facilities.

Table F. RDT Gap Analysis (2015–2017)

Calendar Year	2015	2016	2017
RDT Needs			
Population at Risk	10,300,478	10,630,093	10,970,256
Project % w/ fever (85%[a]) Total number projected fever cases	8,755,406	9,035,579	9,324,718
Percent of fever cases confirmed with microscopy 16.1%[b] (.70*.23)	1,409,620	1,454,728	1,501,279
Percent of fever cases confirmed with RDT 22.8%[c] (.70*32.6)	1,996,232	2,060,112	2,126,036
Consumption data estimate	8,439,689	9,926,842	11,726,298
Total RDT Needs	**8,439,689**	**9,926,842**	**11,726,298**
Partner Contributions			
Government of Benin (HF)	0	0	0
Global Fund/RCC FM/Africare (HF+CH)	390,845	0	0
Global Fund/Round 7/CRS (CH)	269,350	0	0
USG/PMI (HF+CH+PS)	1,700,000	2,000,000	1,800,000
UNICEF (CH)	220,440	220,440	220,440
World Bank (PRSS) (HF,PS,CH)	1,060,000	0	0
New GF (Concept note 40% of total needs)	-	3,970,737	4,690,519
Carryover RDTs	0	0	0
Total RDTs Available	**3,640,635**[1]	**6,191,177**[2]	**6,710,959**[3]
Total RDT Surplus (Gap)	**(4,799,054)**	**(2,675,665)**	**(3,955,339)**

[a,b,c] Based on RMIS, and Facility Health Study estimates of % positivity, % fever, and % facilities capacity to administer RDTs, microscopy.

[1] We assume that the 2015 RDT needs are covered until 43%. Based on the priority which government will give to each level, we can say that community health level needs are totally covered and the health facility level need is partially covered.

[2] We assume that the 2016 RDT needs are covered until 57%. Based on the priority which government will give to each level, we can say that community health level needs are totally covered and the health facility level need is partially covered

[3] We assume that the 2017 RDT needs are covered until 62%. Based on the priority which government will give to each level, we can say that community health level needs are totally covered and the health facility level need is partially covered.

b. ACTs

In this year's MOP, the projected needs include those for the public and private sector (for-profit and not-for-profit) and the community. These figures account for an expected incidence impact from reduced vector presence and diagnostic confirmation at facility and community levels.

Table G. ACT Gap Analysis (2015-2017)

Calendar Year	2015	2016	2017
ACT Needs			
Target population at risk for malaria	10,300,478	10,630,093	10,970,256
Total projected number of malaria cases	5,590,198	5,757,904	5,930,642
Consumption data estimate[1]	5,590,198	5,590,198	5,590,198
Total ACT Needs	**5,590,198**	**5,590,198**	**5,590,198**
Partner Contributions[2]			
ACTs carried over (deficit) from previous year	0	0	0
ACTs from MOH	125,000	125,000	125,000
ACTs from Global Fund	823,217	1,677,059	1,677,059
ACTs from UNICEF	220,440	220,440	220,440
ACTs from World Bank (PRPSS)	1,663,450	0	0
ACTs planned with PMI funding	1,500,000	2,160,000	1,680,000
Total ACTs Available	**4,332,107**	**4,182,499**	**3,702,499**
Total ACT Surplus (Gap)	**(1,258,091)**	**(1,407,699)**	**(1,887,699)**

1. ACT needs are quantified based on consumption data (quantification report 2014) for public, accredited private facilities, and community health workers.
2. The Chinese Embassy also procures antimalarials for Benin; however, as procurement plans are not available in advance, this contribution is not included in this gap analysis.

As shown in the gap table above, only three-quarters of the ACT needs are covered in 2015-2016 and then drops to two-thirds in 2017 due to prioritization of additional ITNs for the universal distribution campaign.

PMI has discontinued the procurement of severe malaria kits, since not all essential items could be provided. Currently, hospitals purchase kits directly from CAME. Costs are supported by the national budget and increasingly from PBF revenue, receiving payment of approximately $10.40 and $11.60 per severe child or pregnant woman case treated respectively.

Plans and justification

Using FY 2016 funding, PMI will procure 1.8 million RDTs and 1,650,000 ACTs and contribute to closing the supply gap. To improve the accuracy of the estimated RDT and ACT needs (see Pharmaceutical Management section for further details), monitor planned procurements, and strengthen the supply chain, including provision to CHWs and accredited private clinics. Consistent with the free malaria treatment policy of the GOB, all PMI-procured ACTs and RDTs are provided free of charge to children under five years of age and pregnant women with confirmed malaria. Monitoring of free provision compliance of PMI-funded commodities will be conducted jointly by the service delivery bilateral and the MOH.

The FY 2016 funding will focus on supporting trained providers to improve and maintain their performance, pre-service training, and in-service IMCI training for the public and private sector. With the scaling up of CHWs who are trained to administer RDTs and ACTs in 10 health zones, PMI's plan with FY 2016 funding is to help meet the need for additional RDTs at the community, private and public health facility levels. Access to malaria commodities will be further expanded based on the pilot experience currently under negotiation with the for-profit health clinics. PMI will also take stock of the diagnostic and quality assurance needs to ensure sufficient diagnostic capacity at the health zone and health facility levels. Quality assurance will be supported by integrated supervision of health workers.

Using FY 2016 funding, PMI plans to increase support for health zone-level performance improvement at the management, health provider and community levels, through integrated malaria case management supervision and comprehensive quality assurance approaches, to improve compliance with case management standards and norms nationwide. This includes the development and testing of health zone summary malaria scorecards to improve coverage, frequency, and effectiveness of supervision nationwide and strengthening community case management.

In line with the national scale-up plan, PMI will support the expansion from five to 10 health zones to provide quality iCCM for sick children under five years of age including the adaptation of approaches to improve access to urban and peri-urban poor populations. Awards to local NGOs will cover training, routine supervision, CHW motivation, and supply chain strengthening to improve iCCM services.

Given observed improvements in confirmed case reporting and availability of malaria commodities at health facilities participating in performance-based financing (PBF), PMI is reviewing opportunities to provide complementary malaria programming to achieve efficient, full national scale malaria quality assurance and improvement efforts. The existing system, funded by the Global Fund, the World Bank, GAVI, and the Belgian Technical Cooperation, now covers all 34 health zones with cash transfers to health facilities and workers for validated, confirmed, simple and complicated malaria cases among children under five years of age and pregnant women as well as the provision of SP and ITNs to pregnant women. The malaria component was added in 2014. Under PBF, all participating health facilities are inspected on a monthly basis with the purpose of validating reported service quantities (e.g. confirmed malaria cases treated must have proper documentation in patient registers indicating diagnostic test result and ACT prescribed). Furthermore, joint quality assessments are conducted quarterly by the external validators with health zone supervision team members at all participating health facilities. During these visits, a comprehensive quality checklist is used to assess stock management, completeness of patient registers, clinical case management, service availability, and human resources. While initially plagued by slow reimbursements, the approval process has been streamlined and health facilities are now receiving payments on a quarterly basis. While the rate of performance improvement varies by site, all health facilities have growing quarterly revenue from PBF. Through the quality scoresheet, PBF provides timely information to health zone managers about factors that affect the functionality of low performing health facilities such as staffing, service availability, financial management, drug supply management, and customer satisfaction. There are examples where the department and health zone have worked together to overcome some of these factors, particularly with the redeployment of health workers, the addition of routine vaccination services, and additional supervision.

PMI is documenting current issues and opportunities to strengthen PBF's contribution towards malaria (e.g. sampling corresponding RDTs in validation process, systematically including malaria commodities in supply management assessment) and to mitigate perverse incentives (e.g. inappropriate use of blood smears, hoarding of drugs in warehouse while not available to service providers). The policy environment is prime for contribution from the national malaria control program to improve PBF as a national effort to harmonize approaches and better integrate the approach to improve sustainability. PMI supports the documentation of evaluations and lessons learned of PBF for the benefit of Benin and other countries discussing PBF in the context of malaria.

USAID/Benin does not directly fund PBF; rather it offers complementary health systems strengthening (HSS) investments such as leadership and management development, provider training, strengthening data for decision-making and commodity logistics that enable local health departments to provide quality health services, including malaria. USAID/Benin currently focuses its HSS support to 10 of the 34 health zones with plans to increase geographic coverage in the coming two to three years.

Proposed activities with FY 2016 funding: ($3,583,972)

1. *Procure RDTs*: PMI plans to procure 1.8 million RDTs. However, recognizing the estimated needs for RDTs (and other commodities such as ACTs) are imprecise, PMI will remain flexible about purchasing commodities and might reprogram some of the funds to purchase more or fewer RDTs and ACTs, depending on ongoing assessments. PMI will work with the NCMP and other partners to clarify the true need, better understand RDT usage patterns, and ensure that supplies do not exceed demand. *($884,972)*

2. *Procure ACTs:* PMI will procure approximately 1,650,000 AL treatments for the public and participating accredited private sector facilities providing free treatment to clients. *($1,749,000)*

3. *Support supervision and strengthening of malaria diagnostic activities*: This activity focuses primarily on laboratory workers. Training is provided during supervision visits with feedback given directly and individually to workers, emphasizing implementing policies and standard operating procedures, microscope maintenance, and quality control of slides/RDTs. There will be a focus on enhanced outreach training to improve the skills of health workers and to support supervision that improves the national malaria Quality Assurance /Quality Control (QA/QC) program for laboratory and clinical health workers. This support will be given to mostly public sector health facilities but will also include the registered private sector providers as well. Existing microscopy capacity will be reinforced in hospitals and health facilities. *($200,000)*

4. *Support quality improvement and supervision of health workers at public, private facilities and at the community level:* PMI will provide technical and financial assistance to the Regional and Health Zone Management Teams. The assistance will support conducting regular supportive supervision visits and findings, IMCI, diagnostics, use of the standard malaria supervision module, verification of free treatment, and monitor health facility and community level standard case management quality

improvement activities. This comprehensive system is coordinated by the MOH with technical assistance from PMI. It incorporates training of supervisors (including supervisors of CHWs), developing practical tools, conducting on-the-job observation and refresher training, record-keeping monitoring, and promoting correct use of diagnostic results. *($250,000)*

5. *Support iCCM of malaria, pneumonia, and diarrhea among sick children:* Support local organizations to reinforce CHW networks in the ten selected health zones and strengthen their quality (diagnostics, treatment, referrals) and sustainability. Support will include mapping CHW coverage gaps; training of replacement CHWs as per the national iCCM training curriculum; monitoring performance through case reviews and observation; reinforcing collaboration with local leaders, women's groups, schools, and other social opinion leaders; strengthening routine community reporting; and supply chain and supervision monitoring. *($500,000)*

b. Pharmaceutical Management

NMCP/PMI objectives

The NSP (2011-2018) for pharmaceutical management objectives are to:
- Facilitate the purchase of ACTs, SP, ITNs, and RDTs
- Streamline spending
- Ensure sustainable distribution of essential products
- Encourage proper use of drugs and ITNs
- Monitor and evaluate the process and outcomes of the supply chain of pharmaceutical management

Progress since PMI was launched

The Central Medical Stores (CAME) has been undergoing reforms during the past five years with support from many partners, the most important of which is PMI. The main objective of PMI since its inception in FY 2008 was to use malaria as an entry point to strengthen the supply chain and pharmaceutical system in order to avoid recurrent stockouts or overstocking. PMI has therefore been investing in building the capacity of Benin's CAME and improving its performance to ensure commodity availability at service delivery points. PMI is also facilitating and supporting the collaboration between CAME, the NMCP, and other players in the pharmaceutical management system such as the *Direction des Pharmacies, des Médicaments et Explorations Diagnostiques* (DPMED) and the National Laboratory for Drugs Quality Control. To improve forecasting, PMI is supporting the NMCP and CAME in planning and implementing a malaria LMIS to ensure that adequate stocks of commodities reach the most remote service delivery points in a timely manner.

Progress during the last 12-18 months

During the past 18 months, PMI conducted a review of the national supervision of the LMIS guidelines for malaria commodities. Recommendations from this review included: 1) the central actors at the NMCP, DPMED, and CAME must correctly use Medistock software for forecasting; 2) Medistock should be upgraded to version 5 in order to provide users with the necessary tools to quantify based on consumption data; 3) an early warning system should be set up to assist the National Health Commodities Committee to promptly mitigate stockouts and overstock situations; 4) the NMCP supply chain team should be strengthened by recruiting a logistician and formally installing the Logistics Management Unit (LMU); 5) commodities from various donors should be pooled into one nationally shared commodity stock to improve fluidity of supply; 6) national drug quality assurance guidelines should be completed and disseminated; and 7) more regular supervision and coaching by zonal depot managers with health facility providers is needed. All these recommended actions have been either incorporated in PMI implementing partners' approved workplans or in the NSP.

To improve the availability of malaria commodities for end users, PMI and other donors are contributing to a standard operating procedure to jointly contribute to national malaria needs taking into consideration nationwide forecasting. Discussions among stakeholders are ongoing to validate the approach which aims to improve product availability for the national program and foresees how to prevent stockouts or overstocks in allowing to the Logistics management Unit (LMU) and TWG to be more focused and proactive[11].The DPMED will provide overall oversight while the TWG and the LMU will be responsible for routine monitoring; ARM3 will support this new work up until its completion. Additionally this approach requires that all commodities provided by partners and by the government have to be delivered to CAME on time according to the national quantification and supply plan. As a result, CAME has the responsibility of managing the common commodity stock without distinguishing the source, nor the beneficiaries, but dispatching commodities through the national regular system.

In the past year, reporting of LMIS data has improved, with all the 34 health zones reporting quarterly and 85% of health facilities providing LMIS reports to the health zone. PMI supports Routine Malaria Data Quality audits (RDQA), a tool established by the NMCP's M&E technical working group (M&E TWG) since 2013. These audits facilitate verification of data quality, the management of data across all levels of the health system, the identification of management issues that affect data quality, and recommendations for improvement. The RDQA allows selected health facilities, health zones, and departments to assess the rigor of reported data as well as identify limitations and weaknesses for improvement action (e.g. cutting of blister packs into smaller divisions to cover missing needs of smaller doses, missing data, supervision, application of nonstandard definitions, missing registers and report formats, etc.). For example, in 2014, the RDQA revealed over-reporting of malaria related deaths in two health departments where nearly one quarter (23%) of the declared cases did not meet case classification criteria. To date, there has been a marked reduction in the number of malaria related deaths and improved match with case definitions. Multiple fora are utilized to discuss findings, problem-solve, and follow up including post-site visit debriefings and supervision visits with the department health management team, the M&E TWG quarterly meetings, and the Roll Back Malaria monthly meetings.

Additionally commodity availability has improved as demonstrated on the past two EUVs (June 2014 in Atlantique-Littoral and November 2014 in Atacora-Donga) conducted with PMI's support. The results show that all the 15 health facilities surveyed had ACT drugs available for treatment of uncomplicated malaria. In addition, the EUV results show that 60% of health facilities reported no stockouts of ACTs, 70% of health facilities reported no stockouts of SP and 68% of health facilities reported no stockouts of RDTs. There was a 25 percentage point reduction in stockouts of three days or more in the three months prior, of all types of ACTs between EUVs conducted in 2014 as compared to 2013.

---

[11] The TWG is functional and regularly holds required quarterly meetings. However, its performance level is low due to weak leadership. The PMI Benin team is advocating for the installation of an LMU comprised of NMCP and PTFs to provide support that is more regular to the NMCP such as routine LMIS data analysis, oversight, and communication with the field. The LMU should have regular meetings at least once per month to work on data and provide inputs to the TWG to prevent crises. While the LMU exists, it is not formally recognized and its meetings are ad hoc in response to urgent issues.

To improve supply chain and pharmaceutical system management, PMI will support CAME to conduct a system assessment using FY 2014 funds in July/August 2015. The objectives of the assessment are to identify opportunities and challenges to the supply chain and distribution systems at the health zone level to ensure availability of commodities at the health facility level, and promote supply chain coordination between central and operational levels. This will also serve to inform the new development plan CAME is writing. The current plan will end in 2015. PMI, in collaboration with other donors, will support the development process as well as its implementation.

Despite the construction of a 32,000 square meter central level warehouse and efforts to create additional regional warehouses, insufficient storage spaces are still a major challenge for CAME. However, CAME now only rents seven offsite spaces compared with 17 when the reform started in 2009. CAME is also preparing the renewal of its partnership agreement with the GOB as the current agreement will expire in 2015. PMI and other partners will support this process in order to maintain the current achievements and avoid any setbacks.

Nationally, the GOB, through CAME, distributes and guarantees the quality of ACTs to public and some private health centers. However, there is little regulatory oversight of ACTs distributed outside the public sector and although over 40% of the population seeks healthcare at private facilities, only 12% of private service providers are registered with the GOB. An abundance of SSFFC is often accessible through the informal sector (at both unregistered private health facilities and local markets). To help combat the low cost counterfeit malarial medications and inform the public on the dangers of illicit ACTs, PMI, in collaboration with the Office of the Inspector General, are supporting the GOB through a United States Private Voluntary Organization and its local affiliate. The support proposes an integrated approach of two communications campaigns over the course of one year (CY 2015) targeting purchasers of antimalarials and drug sellers. In the first campaign, PMI partners will employ several strategies such as a support hotline and targeting entrepreneurs that sell counterfeit ACTs in the second campaign. This one-year campaign will initially target one of the biggest West African markets (Dantokpa Market) and its neighborhood; later rapidly shifting to other markets nationwide identified as particularly problematic.

Plans and justification

FY 2016 funds will be used to continue building country-level partner capacity to better forecast, track, and store malaria commodities. The LMU and the supply chain management TWG will reinforce supervision of the LMIS to improve data completeness, quality, and reporting on commodity availability at the health facility level. PMI will continue to support the national laboratory in quality control testing of malaria commodities at both the port of entry and through spot checks at health facilities. A national supply chain assessment will be conducted in 2015 in partnership with CAME, DPMED, and the National Directorate of Public Health. The NMCP will use the findings to establish supply chain management priorities. Other specific interventions will be defined based on the findings of this assessment.

Proposed activities with FY 2016 funding: ($663,000)

   1. Strengthen LMIS and supply chain management: Based on the recommendations from the 2015 supply chain management assessment, funding will be used to support specific interventions, such as strengthening DPMED, CAME's regional offices and zonal depots, and the logistics information system. Support to strengthen LMIS and the supply chain management system will focus more on the department and zone levels but will continue at all system levels. Depending on specific recommendations, support will be used to improve communications on consumption and stocks from health facility to district and higher levels. Funding will also help develop an integrated waste management plan and strategy for improving the central and decentralized system and to manage the disposal of malaria commodities. *($500,000)*

2. Supervise and monitor the redesigned LMIS: PMI will assist with routine LMIS supervision by the NMCP and departments in the health zones, including the health centers. This includes capacity building at the department and zonal levels. (Supervision within health zones is covered under case management quality improvement). *($33,000)*

3. Test and control drug quality: PMI will provide support to the national laboratory to conduct quality control through routine testing of malaria commodities entering the port and spot checks at public and private facilities. This includes the cost of reagents, equipment for testing, and Minilabs®. *($130,000)*

5. Health system strengthening and capacity building

NMCP/PMI objectives

PMI supports a broad array of health system strengthening activities that cut across intervention areas, such as training of health workers, supply chain management, health information system strengthening, drug quality monitoring, and NCMP capacity building.

The revised Benin NSP (2011-2018) aims at reducing the number of malaria cases by 75% by 2018, using the year 2000 as baseline. In the last five years, the NMCP and PMI have focused on three major challenges within Benin's health system: (1) the lack of adequate human resource capacity (both in numbers and skills sets), to plan, manage, and coordinate a comprehensive malaria program; (2) the collection, management, and use of health information for M&E and surveillance purposes; and (3) supply chain management, which is especially weak at the peripheral level, resulting in recurrent stockouts, and expiration of drugs and RDTs. With these priorities in mind, PMI has worked in close collaboration with the GOB and other stakeholders (WHO, the Global Fund, UNICEF, bilateral partners, and NGOs) to reduce these barriers and reinforce the delivery of malaria interventions. PMI's support in strengthening the health system and the integration of malaria interventions with other programs has benefitted other MOH units and health programs, especially child and maternal health. PMI's HSS work in Benin is fully aligned to the 2008-2018 PNDS components of investing in human resources, strengthening health sector financing, and management. Every effort is made to harmonize malaria investments in HSS within health management and logistics information, and human resources for health systems nationally. USAID/Benin with PMI is actively involved in the development of national norms for community health, including malaria diagnostics and treatment at the community level. Our work at the community level is aligned with the new community health policy expected to be released in June 2015.

With the Global Fund, PMI in Benin is one of the primary partners supporting Benin's health system, using malaria as an entry point. Also supporting Benin's health system are the *Coopération Technique Belge*, the World Bank, the African Bank Development, UNICEF, the Global Alliance for Vaccines and Immunizations, and more recently, the *Coopération Française*, through their recently approved Muskoka Initiative. Key components of PMI's support to the health system include reinforcing health zone management teams' capacity to coordinate service delivery in health facilities and at the community level. PMI has also engaged in supporting the HMIS through building an RMIS that provides accurate data for decision-making. The GOB is still engaged in promoting universal health care financing through the *Régime d'Assurance Maladie Universelle* (RAMU), which is a new MOH priority yet to be fully implemented. To achieve the target of the Millennium Development Goals 4 and 5, the GOB made malaria case management free of charge for children less than five years of age. The GOB expected RAMU to increase access to malaria treatment services, however, RAMU debilitated the drug supply chain since some health facilities do not generate enough income from malaria commodities to cover the cost of providing free medicine to all clients. As a result, this has created stockouts of malaria commodities at health facilities and made forecasting, based on consumption data, more difficult.

PMI's support to health system strengthening and capacity building focuses on improving leadership, management, and governance of the NMCP as a functional unit within the MOH. Support to the department-level malaria staff focuses on data quality, data analysis, and supply chain management. Integrated community case management is implemented by local organizations that are funded from both PMI and USAID/Benin's Maternal and Child Health and Family Planning funding streams.

Progress since PMI was launched
PMI directly invests in government and local organizations where capacity to manage funds is justified. Direct government investment for malaria control efforts is targeted towards the NMCP. Over the past five years, PMI has invested in activities addressing the 2009 organizational capacity assessment recommendations, including human resources, RMIS and information technology, donor coordination, and supply chain management. As a result of PMI's support to the supply chain management, CAME now has a well-functioning board composed of USAID, technical and financial partners, pharmacists, public health professionals, civil society organizations, and the private sector.

PMI investment has focused on capacity building since its start. This includes training of health workers in health facilities and CHWs as well as some medical equipment to health facilities and hospitals. It also includes support for various training provided to NMCP staff members either on technical interventions or on leadership development in order to enable them to effectively accomplish their responsibilities.

The Peace Corps established the Benin Against Malaria (BAM) committee to provide support to all PC volunteers to reduce the burden of malaria by working in their communities to implement malaria prevention activities. The following activities that Peace Corps has completed represent a brief demonstration of the PMI investment and the progression of the Peace Corps towards increased collaboration with the NCMP, a greater contribution as a stakeholder in the fight against malaria in Benin and, a more significant role as a partner with PMI:

- Conducted community-driven needs assessments across the country to help address unidentified gaps in bed net coverage and use

- Assisted the NMCP in malaria activities including the 2014 national bed net distribution, using standardized tools to help inform PMI and NMCP of malaria practices at the village level

- Promotion of malaria prevention in many ways (e.g. National Malaria Day, secondary school curriculum around malaria prevention & treatment as part of a two-week lesson plan)

Progress during the last 12-18 months

During the last 18 months, PMI has supported training activities on each malaria technical intervention. This included the training of over 1,300 health workers in IPTp, surpassing the initial target of 1,176 health workers. In addition, 1,546 health workers were trained in malaria laboratory diagnostics or microscopy, representing 93% of the target (1,749). For treatment, PMI supported the training of 2,610 health workers to correctly administer ACT drugs, which represents 98% of the 2,657 targeted health workers.

PMI supported the implementation of iCCM initiatives in five health zones in northern Benin in collaboration with the MOH, five NGOs, and a network of CHWs. Activities resulted in:

- Reinforced capacity of the local NGOs to supervise CHWs and report iCCM data by training 19 master trainers and 148 heads of health facilities as trainers.

- Developed a joint implementation plan, trained and equipped 1,214 CHWs in the complete package of high impact interventions (malaria, pneumonia, and diarrhea), in collaboration with UNICEF and Global Fund. In addition, 1,500 community health workers were trained to provide malaria case management services to the population. This activity will expand as PMI plans to support the NMCP to train at least 1,000 CHWs annually over the next three years.

PMI is assisting Peace Corps' proposal to NMCP to implement a community based pilot intervention (PecaPalu) that promotes early and active detection and treatment of children under the age of five with malaria.

To contribute to improving malaria diagnosis, PMI continued supporting outreach training and supportive supervision (OTSS). The number of health facilities with laboratories that performed correct malaria diagnostics increased from 81% (41 health facilities out of the 48 having received OTSS supervision) in 2013 to 93% (67 health facilities out of 70 having received OTSS supervision) in 2014.

In accordance with a memorandum of understanding signed between PMI, an implementing partner, and management teams in the 34 health zones, PMI sponsored the training and supervision of 561 health facilities in 27 health zones. This PMI-funded effort also used the collaborative approach to improve the quality of case management in 17 health facilities in Abomey-Calavi and So-Ava, two well-populated areas outside the economic capital of Cotonou.

In the last 18 months, PMI supported the NMCP to strengthen its partnerships with the private sector by providing training for 289 private sector health workers from the Benin Health NGOs Network, the Faith-Based Clinics Association, and Private Clinics Association networks, on malaria diagnostics and case management. With PMI's support, updates were made to the malaria training curricula at Parakou University (a major institution in Benin), and 33 faculty members were trained. PMI facilitated the registration of 80 private clinics and evaluated an additional 99 new health facilities for registration and accreditation by the MOH.

PMI support continued with the revival of the TWGs: M&E, supply chain management, BCC, case management, and vector surveillance. Some PMI implementing partners have made changes in leadership that will enable PMI to increase its technical assistance and facilitate greater Resident Advisor engagement at the NMCP office. There is also more visible participation of NMCP staff in PMI quarterly program reviews, the MOP planning exercise, the Integrated Annual Work Plan workshop and other malaria meetings. Additionally, PMI significantly contributed to the review and finalizing of the

NSP (2011-2018) as well as the development of the concept note for the new funding model of the Global Fund.

With regard to improving the health information system, PMI continued to support the NMCP in implementing the recommendations of the 2013 evaluation of the HMIS. Some of the findings included: lack of a centralized database at the NMCP; different health information databases stored on the personal computers of staff; inconsistency in data collection for some databases; and a low level of motivation among staff responsible for collecting data. PMI continues to support improvements in the system including the provision of internet connection and updated hardware at the NMCP and the continued training of personnel responsible for data collection, management and reporting.

Finally, PMI continued to facilitate the working relationships between the NMCP and CAME by assisting with a review of current plans and helping with the development of better stock tracking tools. These continuous actions have enhanced the NMCP's ability to identify current weaknesses, thereby allowing them to propose actions to remedy them in a timely manner. Recent EUVs have shown that the tracking tools are contributing to improvements in supply chain performance and the distribution of commodities to the peripheral levels. However, free commodities present a particular challenge to supply chain in Benin as they do not receive priority for resupply at the health facility level. The national supply chain assessment planned for 2015 will assess this issue closely and establish recommendations specific to remedying the situation.

PMI team members are directly engaged in NMCP TWGs based on their area(s) of expertise, and actively participate in health sector reviews, malaria strategic planning, and annual integrated malaria plan development and reviews. The two PMI Resident Advisors are based at the USAID health office but also sit at the PMI office within the NMCP.

Plans and justification

In FY 2016, PMI will continue focusing on improving capacity within the MOH in the areas of leadership, management, and governance. In addition, PMI will continue dialogue with the MOH to identify key staff to collaborate with the NMCP to improve leadership across NMCP functions: coordination, information systems, supply chain management, communications, case management, and program development. Furthermore, PMI will continue negotiating with the NMCP to update the assessment conducted in 2008 and implement any recommendations that will improve the management of the program. Such an assessment will include a thorough review of training provided to the NMCP staff since the World Bank Malaria Booster Program started in 2006 and PMI's inception in FY 2008 and recommendations for an innovative and strategic approach to capacity building. PMI has engaged in ongoing dialogue with the NMCP to agree on a better strategy for capacity building. This new approach has influenced FY 2014 reprogramming requests, and FY 2015 pipeline. The FY 2016 funding will complement this strategy by addressing barriers to the NMCP achieving the objectives set forth in the revised NSP (2011-2018). PMI will continue to assist and support the Peace Corps work on malaria control and prevention at the community level and assist the NMCP to provide services to hard-to-reach populations and to identify unmet needs.

The combined effect of these HSS and capacity building activities will enable the NMCP to shape, own, manage, and monitor malaria services at the central, health zone, and health center levels.

Proposed activities with FY 2016 funding: ($120,000)

1. *Support capacity building of the NMCP:* PMI will continue supporting strategic and integrated planning with partners, strengthening the management of TWGs, and logistics support for monthly

45

RBM meetings. PMI will also provide short-term human resources support (specifically, a data manager and accountant). Support will also be provided for NMCP staff field supervision and production of the RMIS data collection tools, LMIS reports, and quarterly bulletin production. Staff training will also be supported per gap analysis as well as attendance to state-of-the-art conferences to make technical presentations on malaria work in Benin. Finally, support will be provided to support running costs of the program's operations along with the GOB and other donors (e.g. internet connection, generator fuel and maintenance, basic office supplies). *($100,000)*

2. *Peace Corps:* Support for two Peace Corps Volunteers (PCVs) who will facilitate malaria BCC activity implementation among Benin PCVs and who will ensure coordination of all malaria efforts carried out by PCVs with PMI and the NMCP. Funding will also be provided to support small grants proposed by PCVs for malaria activities at the community level. *($20,000)*

Table H: Health Systems Strengthening Activities

HSS Building Block Addressed	Technical Area	Description of Activity
Health Services	Case Management	PMI will continue to support improved malaria diagnosis and treatment at the health facility and community levels. PMI will also procure RDTs and ACTs to fill country gaps and monitor commodities distribution as well as quality of drugs.
Health Workforce	Health Systems Strengthening	PMI will continue to build health workforce capacity and maintain support for OTSS. This will continue to improve CHWs' capacity for malaria case management.
Health Information	Monitoring and Evaluation	PMI will support the RMIS to enable the NMCP to collect data for timely decision-making. Also, PMI will continue its support to the commodities tracking tool developed in collaboration with the NMCP and CAME to better monitor stock level.
	Operational Research	PMI core-funds support a net durability study in Seme-Kpodji and strategic modeling of how to use available data for making efficient and impactful decisions. Another OR designed to develop a BCC strategy to promote use of RDTs and acceptability of RDTs at the community level is under implementation in two health zones.
Essential Medical Products, Vaccines, and Technologies	Pharmaceutical management	PMI will support CAME to strengthen the supply chain management and improve forecasting, procurement, quality control, storage and distribution of malaria commodities, such as insecticide-treated nets, artemisinin-based combination therapies and rapid diagnostic tests, mainly at the health zone level.
Health Finance	Public-Private Partnerships	PMI will continue supporting the NMCP to strengthen partnerships with the private sector, including Benin Business Coalition, Faith-based clinics and Benin Health NGO Network to increase their investment in malaria control interventions for staff members and communities they serve.
Leadership and Governance	Health Systems Strengthening	PMI will continue supporting the malaria TWGs (vector control, MIP, case management including community case management, M&E, BCC and supply chain management and drug distribution) as well as Regional Malaria Unit to help improve coordination and communication on strategic guidelines that may affect or induce policy change. PMI partner will work with the NMCP to build leadership and governance capabilities.

6. Behavior Change Communication (BCC)

NMCP/PMI objectives

The national malaria BCC strategy was developed in 2014 as part of the NSP (2011-2018). It is designed to serve as an integrated communication plan, promoting standardized key messages and tools for all malaria partners in Benin. The strategy has identified the following universal BCC target indicators for both urban and rural populations:

- 100% of heads of households know that ITNs are an effective means of prevention against malaria
- 100% of mother and/or child caregivers know the treatment for uncomplicated malaria
- 100% of mother and/or child caregivers know that treatment with ACTs requires positive confirmation with RDTs
- 100% of mothers and/or caregivers know the signs of malaria
- 100% of pregnant women are aware of IPTp and its advantages

The National Integrated Communication Plan for Maternal, Newborn, and Infant survival developed in May 2014 is a four-year plan (2014-2018) intended to improve uptake of malaria interventions, particularly ITNs for pregnant women, newborns and infants and prompt care-seeking for a sick child. The document is structured around documented determinants of health behaviors in Benin. It is designed to be used as a planning tool at the commune level with local government and civil society partners. The national plan includes a full monitoring and evaluation framework with strategic measures from output to impact levels. While the emphasis is on caretaker and health provider knowledge, measures include timely care-seeking, functionality of the referral/counter-referral system, demonstrated capacity in planning and social mobilization at the operational level, training of providers in reception, interpersonal communications, as well as financial resource allocation to health communications.

Progress since PMI was launched

The 2011-2012 DHS results have shown an improvement of behaviors around the use of ITNs with the percentage of those who slept under an ITN the night before the survey increasing among both pregnant women (from 20% in 2006 to 75% in 2011-2012) and children less than five years of age (from 20% in 2006 to 70% in 2011-2012). The uptake of two or more doses of SP is also increasing (from 3% to 23% from the 2006 to 2011-2012 [DHS] and from 28% to 43% from 2011 to 2014 [RMIS]). Prompt care-seeking of children with fever had been stagnant (from <1% in 2006 to 12% in 2012) but limited data from community health interventions shows good uptake of testing and treatment for child malaria cases.

While the DHS did not measure malaria knowledge, PMI supported a recent malaria BCC impact study comparing awareness among 482 mothers of children under five in a full BCC package health zone with a control area in early 2015. The preliminary results indicate high levels of awareness that mosquitoes cause malaria (95% in intervention area; 92% in control), that sleeping under a mosquito net prevents malaria (93% in intervention area; 84% in control); and that fever is a main symptom of malaria (72% in intervention area; 58% in control). However, familiarity with ACT as an effective drug to treat malaria is lower (47% in intervention area; 27% in control). Further results are expected later this year following national review and validation of findings.

PMI supports a multi-pronged approach to reach all segments of the population, including those who are illiterate, through multiple channels including mass media spots on national television and radio featuring malaria music videos, social mobilization events using community theatre, social marketing, as well as interpersonal communications through health facility staff, CHWs, and social and opinion leaders. Reality radio talk shows air on national and local radio. Highly visible flyers are produced on IPTp and SP, ITN use, and treatment of confirmed malaria cases with ACTs. PMI provides technical assistance in the production of radio programs including the monitoring and supervision of recording, editing, and airing. Furthermore, radio stations have guidelines to ensure appropriate and consistent messages. However, more systematic monitoring of BCC activities beyond process indicators is still required.

PMI has supported the revitalization of the NMCP's malaria communications TWG. The group is responsible for reviewing the technical content of all malaria BCC messages and updating the national malaria communications strategy. Group membership is broad, including financial, technical, and implementing partners including the World Bank, UNICEF, WHO, Africare, Catholic Relief Services, PMI, *Association Béninoise du Marketing Social*, and the Peace Corps.

For communication activities specifically related to IRS, PMI adopted a streamlined approach under which the majority of spray operators are also engaged in community mobilization, structure identification, and enumeration activities.

In 2012, PMI conducted IPTp formative research, which identified a number of sociocultural issues including low awareness of the advantages of receiving SP, perceived negative consequences of taking SP during pregnancy by both mothers and health workers, and poor quality of reception at ANC consultations. Mass media and interpersonal communication channels are important tools for addressing perceptions and attitudes about SP during pregnancy. Interpersonal communications interventions with health providers in Benin has shown some improvement in client-provider reception.

PMI supports two Child Survival & Health Grants programs in Benin, which are generating evidence for determinants of malaria behaviors. The first focuses on testing local solutions for net durability and for sleeping under ITNs including preventing or repairing damage to nets (e.g. tying up during the day, storing away from food, avoiding tears during drying, keeping away from fire, etc.). The second focuses on prompt care-seeking for sick children, the acceptability of RDTs by mothers, and compliance with RDT results at the community level. Both projects are approaching their mid-point of implementation.

Progress during the last 12-18 months

During the last 12-18 months, PMI supported household-level communications that were implemented nationwide. Malaria work plans with BCC activities and sub grants with local organizations were put into place in all 34 health zones to intensify efforts. PMI trained 1,214 CHWs in communication strategies in order to promote the prevention of malaria in pregnancy at the household level; collectively, these CHWs conducted 21,315 home visits. PMI provided support to 19 local radio and two TV stations for programming containing key messages on malaria prevention, diagnosis and case management, and quality of care. These efforts reached an estimated 1,529,500 women and 1,629,500 men every three months. The TV spot on World Malaria Day, which had a targeted focus on SP uptake, aired more than 30 times. Community theatre groups covered five of the six departments with interactive skits on ITN use, SP uptake, prompt care-seeking for malaria and quality health care services; these performances reached an estimated 28,000 individuals, most of which were women. A special campaign was held in

Figneyon, a densely populated, low-income community in Cotonou with low health care access. The event reached over 1,000 people.

PMI has made consistent investments in BCC activities over the past few years but has yet to understand the impact of those investments. In 2014, PMI implementing partners developed an evaluation protocol to provide more scientific evidence in regards to determinants and performance of malaria prevention and care-seeking behaviors. The planned evaluation, which will be carried out in late 2015, will include 400 structured interviews for mothers across 10 health facilities in two to four health departments that received the most intense PMI-supported BCC interventions over the past three years. The tool will measure independent variables (exposure to messages, specific channels, and message recall), intermediate outcomes (malaria knowledge measures), and health outcomes (e.g. slept under an ITN last night, received any IPTp during last pregnancy, received more than one IPTp treatment during last pregnancy, obtained a diagnostic test for malaria, treated confirmed malaria with ACT, etc).

With the heightened concern about SSFFC ACTs on the market in Benin since 2014, PMI, with core support, designed a special communication campaign, targeting urban poor families about the risk associated with purchasing ineffective medicines and the benefits of testing before treating suspected malaria cases. This campaign was carried out over a one-year period in Cotonou. Recall surveys will be conducted in July 2015 to determine the reach of the activity.

Plans and justification

With FY 2016 funding, PMI will support household-level communications on the problem behaviors of prompt care-seeking, including testing for malaria and monthly IPTp, starting early in the second trimester. Support will be maintained for core messaging on the use and maintenance of nets and IRS. Local organizations will be supported to implement the National Malaria BCC Strategy and Integrated Communication Plans at the commune and household level using mixed local media and interpersonal communication. As part of these efforts, a new BCC partner will provide technical assistance to strengthen effectiveness monitoring and decision-making by the BCC TWG to improve the national communications strategy. As the partners in country move forward with collecting BCC data to measure behavior change and demonstrate the value of specific approaches, PMI will encourage and help facilitate the use of PMI resources such as the BCC pilot toolkit.

Proposed activities with FY 2016 funding: ($260,000)

1. *Support community and household-level malaria communication activities:* FY 2016 funds will be used to support BCC activities that promote net use among pregnant women and children under five years of age and the hanging up and maintenance of nets. PMI FY 2016 BCC support will also help improve prompt and appropriate care-seeking behavior and encourage ANC attendance and IPTp uptake until delivery. PMI-supported local organizations working in ten selected health zones will receive technical and financial support to implement national malaria BCC messages and materials using multiple channels including local radio, community theatre, traditional music, local women's groups, as well as interpersonal counseling from health providers and CHWs. *($200,000)*

2. *Technical and financial assistance for national-level communication planning and mass campaigns:* PMI will provide support to plan and deliver national malaria events and special campaigns. *($35,000)*

3. *Technical assistance to strengthen BCC measurement*: PMI will contribute to wider efforts to improve evaluation and documentation of effectiveness of BCC efforts. Funding will provide technical assistance to strengthen national efforts to evaluate and document malaria BCC interventions. *($25,000)*

7. Monitoring and Evaluation

NMCP/PMI objectives

Benin's national malaria M&E strategic plan (2011–2018) is designed to capture malaria trends and describe the dynamics of social, temporal, and spatial distribution of morbidity and mortality. Ideally this information can be used to determine the risk factors for malaria in order to propose prevention measures and appropriate recommendations that inform interventions or assess the prevention activities.

Benin's M&E activities include a multi-institutional M&E TWG and monitoring of programmatic process indicators with routinely collected data and periodic evaluations of outcome indicators. Benin has multiple sources of malaria information, all of which are supported and strengthened by PMI and include: 1) household and health facility surveys; 2) end-use verification surveys; and 3) the national HMIS.

The NMCP's M&E operations have recently transitioned through an interim leadership period and now benefits from the arrival of a new section chief, which will allow greater M&E capacity and more sustained engagement with important M&E activities.

Progress since PMI was launched

Demographic and Health Surveys were completed in 2006 (PMI's baseline survey) and 2011-2012. These DHSs were methodologically similar with two exceptions: 1) the 2006 survey was done at the end of the rainy season and the 2011-2012 survey was done during the dry season, and 2) only the 2011-2012 survey measured parasitemia prevalence. The United Nations Children's Fund (UNICEF) administered a Multiple Indicator Cluster Survey (MICS) in 2014, however, due to timing, PMI was not able to incorporate an expansion of the malaria module to measure biomarkers. Preliminary findings from this survey indicate that the reductions in child mortality rate observed from the 2006 (125 deaths/1,000 live births) to 2011-2012 (70 deaths/1,000 live births) DHS may have been over estimated. The 2014 MICS estimated child mortality at 105 deaths per 1,000 live births. Another nationally representative household survey (the Leadership and Development [LEADD] survey), based on the MIS methodology, was conducted in November 2010. However, methodological concerns and the use of non-standard indicators may have compromised the validity of the results. The NMCP plans to complete an MIS in early 2016. A timely implementation of an MIS in early 2016 would likely delay the DHS until 2018, and would be timed to capture parasitemia (i.e., end of the rainy season).

Results from a PMI-supported ITN durability assessment (completed in 2013)[12] designed to monitor indicators of durability, survivorship, and integrity observed a survivorship closer to a two-year ITN serviceable life assumption as opposed to three years. Additionally, the integrity of nearly one-third of 'surviving' nets was so degraded that they were in need of replacement. As a result of this study, PMI, in collaboration with CREC and the NMCP, will conduct regular Vector Control Work Group meetings to

---

[12]Gnanguenon V, *et al.* 2014. Durability assessment results suggest a serviceable life of two, rather than three, years for the current long-lasting insecticidal (mosquito) net (LLIN) intervention in Benin. BMC Infectious Diseases 14: 69 – 79.

discuss programmatic implications and opportunities, such as increasing BCC strategies to support ITN repair and maintenance and to reinforce available channels for routine replacement of ITNs between national campaigns. There is currently a centrally-funded operational research study underway in Benin that will also help inform PMI on whether certain strategies applied in specific test areas can increase the longevity and utilization of ITNs.

Four of the 11 IRS entomological monitoring sites conducted by CREC continue to monitor vector-insecticide susceptibility, including assessing the longevity of insecticides on the wall. This includes evaluations for the presence of physiological resistance mechanisms in the malaria vector (including mixed function oxidases, a mechanism that, if present, can be managed through the use of new ITN products). PMI will continue to support its existing resistance entomological surveillance and ITN monitoring activities.

In 2009 and 2013, nationally representative health facility surveys were conducted to assess the availability of malaria-related commodities, diagnostic capacity, and quality of malaria case management. Beginning in 2010, EUVs of commodity availability were conducted on a quarterly basis and completed on small convenience samples of health facilities. A larger EUV on a nationally representative sample of 128 health facilities was completed in April 2012. In 2013 and 2014, there was a return to quarterly administered EUVs. However, due to the demands of the national bednet distribution, there were only three EUVs done in 2014.

From 2008 to 2013, PMI funded the Regional Institute of Public Health in Benin to supervise the collection and reporting of data on malaria morbidity and mortality from five hospital sentinel surveillance sites. Data reported from the sites generated tables of key malaria indicators and trend analyses, however, the information generated from the data was not used to inform any programmatic decisions or activities. Evaluations of the sentinel sites showed that relatively low proportions of outpatient cases with suspected malaria were tested (63% in 2010 and 60% in 2011), due in part to the persistent commodity stockouts of RDTs, and ACT presentations at the sites. Additional situational and organizational constraints of the system prompted a PMI/NMCP decision to suspend the surveillance activity in 2014.

The HMIS reports the number of malaria cases, deaths, and case fatality rates at the health facility level on a monthly basis. Prior to PMI, the HMIS did not distinguish clinically diagnosed cases from those confirmed by laboratory testing. In addition, concerns existed about the accuracy, timeliness, and coverage of the data, as well as how the data were used for decision-making. With the support of PMI, the World Bank, and WHO, the NMCP is strengthening the malaria module of the national HMIS (i.e., the Routine Malaria Information System, or RMIS) to achieve the evaluation indicator goal of at least 80% of public and private health facilities continuously and accurately reporting malaria data. Beginning in 2013, quality, timeliness, and completeness of data reporting have improved significantly and the number of health facilities reporting exceeds the desired goal (details below). The system collects and reports on twenty key malaria indicators each month. The module was recently updated to include reports from community health workers; however the precision of confirmed positivity, and the reliability of capturing total health facility new malaria cases remain significant concerns. With support from PMI, quarterly RMIS newsletters are prepared to keep stakeholders abreast of the current malaria epidemiological situation in Benin. However, during the past year, due to a transition in M&E leadership along with parallel responsibilities related to administering a national net campaign, there was a delay in the publication of RMIS bulletins. Current bulletins are used to inform the NMCP, as well as zonal and departmental level M&E and leadership staff on the progress in data collection improvements. The data are also used by the M&E TWG to confirm ongoing data quality needs but they are not timely for informing programmatic decisions. PMI is working with local partners and the M&E TWG to draft concrete next steps for more centralized analyses and for the utilization of RMIS data for decision-making.

Table I. Monitoring and Evaluation Data Sources

Data Source	Activities	Calendar Year (2006-2018)												
		'06	'07	'08	'09	'10	'11	'12	'13	'14	'15	'16	'17	'18
National–level Household surveys	Demographic and Health Survey (DHS)	X						X						X^1
	Multiple Indicator Cluster Survey (MICS)									X^2				
	LEADDS					X								
	MIS											X^3		
Health Facility and Other Surveys	EUV survey					X	X	X	X	X	X	X	X	
	Health facility survey				X					X				
Malaria Surveillance and Routine System Support	Sentinel surveillance						X	X	X	X	X			
	Support to HMIS			X	X	X	X	X	X	X	X	X	X	
	HMIS Evaluation (see HSS section)									X				
Therapeutic Efficacy monitoring	*In vivo* efficacy testing					X					X^4	X	X	
Entomology	Entomological surveillance and resistance monitoring					X	X	X	X	X	X	X	X	
Other Data Sources	Malaria Impact Evaluation												X	

[1] Ongoing discussion with partners regarding finances and year DHS will be conducted
[2] Funding by UNICEF
[3] Funding by the Global Fund
[4] Funding by WHO

Progress during the last 12-18 months

PMI provided the NMCP with technical assistance for its 2014 national net campaign, the M&E components of the NSP (2011-2018), and continues to offer assistance to support higher quality routine data collection as well as improve M&E measures for all activities. There are ongoing discussions regarding ways to contribute easily available information during the IRS campaign that may improve the NMCP's ability to utilize ITN M&E data during national distribution campaigns as well as a practical and valuable M&E component for an upcoming BCC evaluation. This type of information is currently being collected along with household demographic data on at risk populations. Currently there is also a PMI centrally-funded project that uses innovative technology to demonstrate how data can be used to improve decision-making that affects malaria prevention at the community level.

M&E support: During the last 12-18 months, PMI and the NMCP continued to collaborate closely on M&E issues, and PMI Resident Advisors remained active participants in the M&E TWG. The TWG did not meet because of the NMCP's preoccupation with planning for the national net campaign in October 2014. The TWG recently met in 2015 to review, discuss, and plan for an epidemiologic and entomologic paired data analysis. It was agreed that higher quality epidemiologic data are critically needed to achieve a more comprehensive understanding of malaria burden and malaria transmission at the sub-district or sub-department level. Previous evaluations showed that the sentinel surveillance sites did not provide any added value to the existing HMIS/RMIS as this activity did not generate accurate malaria burden data to inform programmatic decisions. The M&E TWG in collaboration with the NMCP decided to invest PMI funds towards strengthening the HMIS/RMIS. In the past year, the RMIS form was updated to include indicators from CHWs. Redirected funds have gone towards trainings and supervision of CHWs and district and health zone coordinators on the RMIS form completion. Additionally, the M&E TWG is continuing to work with the NMCP to look for credible data that can assist all partners to make decisions about ongoing malaria control activities and interventions.

As PMI supports iCCM national scale-up, it is critical to evaluate the performance, costs, challenges, and lessons learned from this intervention. PMI has increased support to health zones based on implications of the free malaria treatment policy. PMI supported the training of 153 CHWs to pilot the collection and transmission of data from five zones offering iCCM in 2009 to 10 zones in 2015, doubling the number of CHWs providing iCCM services. A midterm process evaluation will assess the performance effects of this expansion (more CHWs, and more services, supervision, and reporting into HMIS) as well as review the newer components introduced since the 2012 iCCM evaluation. This transfer included the transfer of management to local organizations, the use of mHealth, and the incorporation of RDTs, as well as data using a new pilot mHealth (SMS) initiative to improve timeliness and quality of data reported to health facilities in two zones (Bassila and Tchaorou). Data from this pilot activity is currently being analyzed. Further, USAID/Benin supported a comprehensive national M&E community health plan that incorporated best practices and global metric standards to harmonize different data collection systems being used. Additional performance evaluation measures are planned, including a 2015 baseline survey and performance evaluation in 2016.

In 2014, PMI supported the development and introduction of a smartphone application for iCCM in the health zones of Tchaourou and Bassila to report on cases seen, referrals, stocks, and routine activities. A total of 46 health workers (including statisticians) and 142 CHWs were trained on the system and 169 mobile phones were distributed to users (CHWs, heads of health facilities, and health zone statisticians). At the end of the year, an assessment of the pilot's effectiveness was conducted to evaluate best practices and lessons learned for all components. The system was widely appreciated by all the zone statisticians and most of the CHWs (e.g., saves time, ease of reporting, collaboration with supervisors) and most users expressed good knowledge of the system and the ability to send reports via the electronic system referred to as CommCare. Challenges were reported in routine daily reporting by CHWs due to limited availability of mobile phones (one per village instead of one per CHW), poor network coverage in some locations, and difficulty in finding a power supply to recharge phones.

Survey Support: PMI continued support of EUVs to gauge commodity availability at health facilities. The most recent EUV conducted in November 2014 in northern Benin noted a continued lack of sufficient and timely reporting on consumption data as well as continued need for additional training in microscopy. Given the slow uptake of case management guidelines, PMI tries to conduct a nationally representative health facility survey every four years to assess the readiness of outpatient health facilities to manage malaria, as well as the quality of malaria case management in outpatient settings, laboratory testing, and antenatal care. The previous health facility survey was conducted in October 2013. Results from the EUVs and the health facility survey showed consistent stockouts of malaria commodities including RDTs, ACTs, and SP. As a result, diagnoses of malaria usually did not follow the national treatment guidelines, which require testing using RDTs when malaria is suspected.

After a several year hiatus of PMI-funded therapeutic efficacy studies (TES) in Benin, the WHO funded the NMCP to implement a TES in two sites in December 2014. This study should end by July 2015. Following recent discussions with WHO and PMI leadership, in future years, TES will be implemented in two to four sites each year with WHO and PMI alternating as partners with the NMCP. PMI will fund TES in two or three sites in calendar year 2016, and discussions of including K13 molecular marking are ongoing.

HMIS Support: During the last 12 months, PMI supported refresher training on the operation and maintenance of the data logic system used in the collection of HMIS and RMIS data for statisticians in the 34 health zones. Quarterly supervision of selected data collection sites in six departments, covering 34 health zones, were conducted in addition to two routine data quality assessment audits designed to improve data collection. PMI provided technical guidance to improve the quality of health facility data reported to the RMIS through quarterly regional validation workshops. From October 2011 to December 2014, the percentage of health facilities submitting complete and timely data on malaria burden indicators increased from 35% to 95%. One semi-annual and one annual RMIS bulletin were published.

Plans and justification

PMI is committed to working with the NMCP to support monitoring the quality of malaria data collected through RMIS to ensure that the programmatic needs of the NMCP are met. The ability to use routine data to identify temporal and geographic variation morbidity or mortality in an endemic country like Benin would be an important milestone to achieve. Support from PMI will contribute to key data collection and analysis activities, including quarterly EUVs and the 2018 DHS, to work towards strengthening the NMCP's M&E strategy. PMI will also provide support to help prepare for an impact evaluation of PMI interventions on all-cause child mortality indicators in Benin.

Proposed activities with FY 2016 funding: ($460,000)

1. *Support routine malaria information system:* PMI will continue support to strengthen procedures and indicators for malaria in the national HMIS and comprehensive strengthening of the overall system. The funding will support the NMCP's efforts to implement PMI's recommendations, in particular: 1) providing training in database management, analysis, and survey methodologies to enhance data accuracy and quality; 2) increased technical assistance and material support to the zonal offices; 3) creation of a final, detailed (and updated) indicator list with better case definitions; and 4) creation and printing of written documentation (i.e., standard operating procedures, protocols) with specific tasks, dates, and persons responsible for all levels participating in the RMIS. *($250,000)*

2. *Funding to gather data and provide technical assistance for upcoming PMI Benin Impact Evaluation:* PMI support will help prepare for an upcoming impact evaluation. *($100,000)*

3. *Conduct EUV surveys:* FY 2016 funds will continue to support quarterly monitoring of the availability and utilization of key antimalarial commodities at the health facility level. *($100,000)*

4. *Technical assistance:* PMI will provide technical assistance from the CDC PMI M&E team. Technical assistance will include working with the NMCP to support strengthening RMIS. *($10,000)*

8. Operational research

NMCP/PMI objectives

The NSP (2011-2018) reiterates the importance of conducting operational research (OR) as an essential strategy to measure impact of control and prevention activities, and to identify gaps and weaknesses to improve program implementation. Since Benin became a PMI focus country in 2008, OR has been integral in evaluating the efficacy of vector control strategies and assessing approaches to addressing malaria program deficiencies.

Progress since PMI was launched

With strong collaboration with CREC and the NMCP, multiple studies have been completed in Benin and have helped inform vector control strategies in various other PMI focus countries. In light of the increased resistance to pyrethroid insecticides used on ITNs, Benin completed a cluster randomized controlled study to examine the effectiveness of combining ITNs and IRS (using bendiocarb) to ITNs and carbamate-treated plastic sheeting (CTPS), to full coverage with ITNs and the usual coverage as per NMCP policy (as the control arm). The primary endpoint was the incidence density rate of *Plasmodium falciparum* clinical malaria in children under six years of age. Clinical and parasitological information were obtained by active case detection of malaria episodes during 12 periods of six consecutive days scheduled at six weekly intervals and by cross-sectional surveys of asymptomatic plasmodial infections. Results showed that households with IRS and ITNs or IRS and CPTS had lower entomological inoculation rates (EIRs) of 4.3 compared to 8 and 7.2 for the full coverage with ITN and control arms respectively. Clinical cases of malaria decreased from 2.5 to 1.8 cases per child/year after IRS implementation. The use of IRS with a non-pyrethroid was successful in decreasing EIRs compared to communities using only ITNs.[13]

Another OR study completed in 2009, assessed a colorimetric test in comparison with the standard WHO cone bioassay test for insecticidal activities of deltamethrin. New and used/previously washed nets were tested by both the WHO cone bioassay and the colorimetric test. Results showed that the colorimetric test had a sensitivity of 93% and a specificity of 87% of accurately assessing levels of deltamethrin on ITNs, compared to the cone bioassay.[14]

---

[13] Corbel V, *et al.* 2012. Combination of malaria vector control interventions in pyrethroid resistance area in Benin: a cluster randomized controlled trial. Lancet Infect Dis, 12: 617-26.

[14] Green M, *et al.* 2009. Rapid colorimetric field test to determine levels of deltametrhin on PermaNet surfaces: association with mosquito bioactivity. Trop Med Int Heal, 14: 381-88.

National ITN distribution every three years is a key intervention in Benin's malaria control strategy. Data from the field indicate that ITN lifespan appears to vary according to intrinsic and extrinsic factors. In collaboration with CREC, PMI provided technical assistance to monitor two indicators of ITN durability: survivorship and integrity, to validate the three-year serviceable life assumption. Results showed that observed survivorship, after 18 months, was significantly less ($p<0.0001$) than predicted, based on the assumption that nets last three years. Rather, predicted survivorship was closer to a two-year ITN serviceable life assumption ($p=0.03$). Five factors were associated with degraded nets (loss of fabric integrity): washing frequency, proximity to water for washing, location of kitchen, type of cooking fuel, and low net maintenance. The main recommendation was that a two-year serviceable life for the current ITN intervention in Benin would be more programmatically efficient.[15]

Progress during the last 12-18 months

A study to determine the operational feasibility of using dried tube specimens (DTS) as quality control and proficiency testing samples for malaria RDTs was completed in January 2015. Dried tube specimens and RDTs were stored at a reference laboratory and were compared to DTS and RDTs stored at two health facilities to determine the ability of DTS to detect facility RDTs and also how quality control based on DTS can be incorporated into a larger RDT quality assurance program. Dried tube specimens showed expected results throughout the study period, however, indications were that DTS were more stable under refrigeration. Programmatic implications suggest that DTS can be successfully implemented as a quality control method for RDTs in the field. This quality control may increase health worker confidence in the test result, thereby increasing the proportion of suspected malaria cases that are confirmed by a test and also decrease antimalarial drug prescription to patients who test negative by RDTs.

Recent studies of LLINs under field conditions have shown that the deterioration of the physical condition of the nets is often the limiting factor and in many cases, nets were worn out before three years. To encourage innovation in LLIN technology, textile engineers have developed resistance to damage (RD) scores that are based upon laboratory tests designed to mimic the primary causes of damage under field conditions. The aim is to encourage innovation in LLINs to increase their field longevity and reduce the cost per year of protection. Current LLIN products have been tested and ranked using this methodology. Using core PMI FY 2014 and FY 2015 funding, Benin has begun validating RD scores of six different LLINs, including two products with modified net structures (e.g. increased fabric weight, different knitting patterns) designed to increase their resistance to damage. The data generated by the study is expected to validate the RD scores as predictors of field durability, allow for differential pricing of long-lasting ITNs based upon their RD scores and ultimately to spur innovation among industry to develop newer, longer lasting LLINs.

---

[15] Gnanguenon V, *et al*. 2014. Durability assessment results suggest a serviceable life of two, rather than three, years for the current long-lasting insecticidal (mosquito) net (LLIN) intervention in Benin. BMC Infectious Diseases 14: 69 – 79.

Table J. PMI-funded Operational Research Studies

Completed OR Studies			
Title	**Start date (est.)**	**End date (est.)**	**Budget**
Implementation of a vector control strategy based on a combination of a pyrethroid ITN + a non-pyrethroid IRS at the community level to assess its protective efficacy against malaria in an area where *Anopheles gambiae s.s.* has a high level of pyrethroid resistance.	4/2008	10/2011	$300,000
Evaluation of a new technology (colorimetric test) for determining when to replace ITNs in communities	06/2008	03/2009	$37,000
Durability assessment of long-lasting insecticide-treated mosquito nets in Benin	07/2011	07/2013	$200,000
Field testing of dried malaria-positive blood as quality control samples for malaria RDTs	05/2014	01/2015	$25,000
Ongoing OR Studies			
Correlating resistance to damage (RD) scores with long-lasting insecticide-treated net performance and longevity in various field conditions in Africa	09/2015	09/2017	
Planned OR Studies FY 2016			
Title	**Start date (est.)**	**End date (est.)**	**Budget**
No planned OR activities			

Proposed activities with FY 2016 funding: ($0)
There are no planned OR activities with FY 2016 funding.

9. Staffing and administration

Two health professionals serve as resident advisors to oversee PMI in Benin, one representing CDC and one representing USAID. In addition, one or more Foreign Service Nationals (FSNs) work as part of the PMI team. All PMI staff members are part of a single interagency team led by the USAID Mission Director or his/her designee in country. The PMI team shares responsibility for development and implementation of PMI strategies and work plans, coordination with national authorities, managing collaborating agencies and supervising day-to-day activities. Candidates for resident advisor positions (whether initial hires or replacements) will be evaluated and/or interviewed jointly by USAID and CDC, and both agencies will be involved in hiring decisions, with the final decision made by the individual agency.

The PMI professional staff work together to oversee all technical and administrative aspects of the PMI, including finalizing details of the project design, implementing malaria prevention and treatment activities, monitoring and evaluation of outcomes and impact, reporting of results, and providing guidance to PMI partners.

The PMI lead in country is the USAID Representative. The day-to-day lead for PMI is delegated to the USAID Health Office Director and thus the two PMI resident advisors, one from USAID and one from CDC, report to the USAID Health Office Director for day-to-day leadership, and work together as a part of a single interagency team. The technical expertise housed in Atlanta and Washington guides PMI programmatic efforts.

The two PMI resident advisors are based within the USAID health office and are expected to spend approximately half their time sitting with and providing technical assistance to the national malaria control programs and partners.

Locally-hired staff to support PMI activities either in Ministries or in USAID will be approved by the USAID Mission Director. Because of the need to adhere to specific country policies and USAID accounting regulations, any transfer of PMI funds directly to Ministries or host governments will need to be approved by the USAID Mission Director and Controller, in addition to the US Global Malaria Coordinator.

Proposed activities with FY 2016 funding: ($1,990,048)

>   *1. USAID staff and other in-country administrative expenses:* Support for one USAID PMI Advisor, foreign national malaria dedicated and cross-cutting staff, and other administrative local costs to USAID/Benin, including ICASS costs. *($1,612,048)*
>
>   *2. CDC technical staff:* Support one resident advisor. *($378,000)*

Table 1: Budget Breakdown by Mechanism
President's Malaria Initiative – Benin
Planned Malaria Obligations for FY 2016

Partner	Geographic Area	Activity	Budget ($)	%
TBD – Supply Chain Contract	Nationwide	Procure ITNs, SP, RDTs, and ACTs	$9,592,952	58%
IRS 2 IQC/ Task Order 6	IRS prioritized communes	Technical assistance, procurement, implementation of IRS, and environmental compliance	$2,100,000	13%
USAID	Nationwide	USAID technical staff and in-country support to PMI	$1,612,048	10%
New Mission Bilateral Program	Nationwide	IPTp and case management performance improvement, strengthening malaria diagnostic activities, malaria training, national BCC technical assistance	$779,000	5%
Local NGOs Community PIHI	Ten Health Zones	Support iCCM and BCC in 10 selected health zones using local community organizations	$700,000	4%
SIAPS	Nationwide	Strengthen LMIS, supply chain management, and conduct EUVs	$600,000	4%
CDC Interagency Agreement	Nationwide	Technical assistance for IRS and M&E	$45,000	3%

Partner	Geographic Area	Activity	Budget ($)	%
	Cotonou	One Resident Advisor	$378,000	
National Malaria Control Program	Nationwide	Capacity building, RMIS, LMIS, and IRS supervision and monitoring	$383,000	2%
CREC	Nationwide	Implementation of some IRS and entomologic surveillance	$160,000	1%
USP PQM	Nationwide	Drug quality control testing	$130,000	1%
Peace Corps	Nationwide	Support volunteers and community- and facility-based malaria activities	$20,000	<1%
TOTAL			**$16,500,000**	**100%**

Table 2: Budget Breakdown by Activity
President's Malaria Initiative - Benin
Planned Malaria Obligations for FY 2016

Proposed Activity	Mechanism	Budget Total $	Budget Commodity $	Geographic Area	Description
PREVENTIVE ACTIVITIES					
Insecticide-treated Nets					
Procure and distribute routine ITNs	TBD - Supply Chain Contract	$2,281,980	$2,281,980	National	Procure and deliver to health facilities approximately 520,000 LLINs for routine distribution through ANC and EPI services.
Procure and distribute universal campaign ITNs	TBD - Supply Chain Contract	$4,380,000	$4,380,000	National	Procure and pre-position approximately 1,000,000 ITNs to health facilities for the 2017 national net campaign.
SUBTOTAL ITNs		**$6,661,980**	**$6,661,980**		
Indoor Residual Spraying					
IRS implementation and management	IRS 2 Task Order 6 and MOH	$2,100,000	$0	Prioritized IRS communes	In collaboration with CREC, NMCP, MOH district and local authorities, and with continued focus on building capacity, support IRS implementation in designated communes. IRS operations include training of personnel, purchase of insecticide and related spray equipment, community mobilization, and implementation.

Proposed Activity	Mechanism	Budget		Geographic Area	Description
		Total $	Commodity $		
Entomological monitoring for spray areas and selected sentinel sites	CREC	$160,000	$0	National	Entomological monitoring and surveillance of vectors for insecticide resistance, in spray areas and in sentinel sites. CREC will work with NMCP staff trained in entomology.
Procure vector control supplies	CDC IAA	$6,000	$0	National	Procure equipment and replacement supplies for insectary, traps, spray and landing catches, storage of specimens, and related laboratory supplies.
Technical assistance for entomological capacity building	CDC IAA	$29,000	$0	National	Funding for two technical assistance visits from CDC to monitor IRS and entomologic surveillance.
SUBTOTAL IRS		**$2,295,000**	**$0**		
Malaria in Pregnancy					
Procurement of SP	TBD - Supply Chain Contract	$297,000	$297,000	National	Procure approximately 1.65 million treatments of SP (3 doses) to contribute to supporting all projected pregnancies. SP will be made available to both the public and private sector.
Support supervision and refresher training	New bilateral	$169,000	$0	National	Support on-site supervision and refresher training of health care workers including benchmark assessments, on-the-spot training and coaching for improved quality of service in MIP and case management.
SUBTOTAL MIP		**$466,000**	**$297,000**		
SUBTOTAL PREVENTIVE		**$9,422,980**	**$6,958,980**		

Proposed Activity	Mechanism	Budget		Geographic Area	Description
		Total $	Commodity $		
CASE MANAGEMENT					
Procurement of RDTs	TBD - Supply Chain Contract	$884,972	$884,972	National	Procure approximately 1,800,000 RDTs for use in health facilities and in communities via CHWs to cover most of the nationwide needs.
Procure ACTs	TBD - Supply Chain Contract	$1,749,000	$1,749,000	National	Procure approximately 1,650,000 AL treatments which is about 25% of the projected need based on consumption data.
Support supervision and strengthen malaria diagnostics	New bilateral	$200,000	$0	National	Support supervision and monitoring of malaria diagnostics, maintenance of microscopes, training, and quality control of slides/RDTs at the health facility and community levels.
Support quality improvement and supervision of health workers	New bilateral	$250,000	$0	National	Provide support to departments and health zones to conduct on-site supervision of health workers including benchmark assessments, on-the-spot training and coaching, supervision of clinical, diagnostic activities, and logistics activities.
Support community case management	Local NGO Community PIHI Support Grants	$500,000	$0	Targeted health zones	Support an iCCM program in 10 selected health zones, which complements the Global Fund, UNICEF, and World Bank iCCM program to provide full national coverage.
Strengthen logistics management information system and supply chain management	Systems for Improved Access to Pharmaceuticals and Services (SIAPS)	$500,000	$0	National	Based on assessment recommendations, conduct specific interventions, such as strengthening DPMED, CAME's regional offices and zonal depots and the logistics

Proposed Activity	Mechanism	Budget		Geographic Area	Description
		Total $	Commodity $		
					information system.
LMIS supervision	NMCP	$33,000	$0	National	Routine LMIS supervision from NMCP and departments to the health zones, including the health centers. (Supervision within health zones covered under case management quality improvement).
Drug quality control testing	USP PQM	$130,000	$0	National	Provide support to the national laboratory for quality control to conduct routine testing of ACTs entering the port and spot checks at public and private facilities. Support the cost of reagents and equipment for testing.
SUBTOTAL CASE MANAGEMENT		**$4,246,972**	**$2,633,972**		
HEALTH SYSTEM STRENGTHENING / CAPACITY BUILDING					
Support capacity building of the NMCP	NMCP	$100,000	$0	Central	Direct support for strategic and integrated planning with partners, management of technical working groups, human resource capacity building (e.g. data manager, accountant), staff training as per a gap analysis, some sponsorship for participation in international conferences, and some NMCP operational running cost gaps (i.e. internet, fund for generator maintenance and fuel).
Peace Corps Response Volunteers and Small Project Grants	Peace Corps	$20,000	$0	NA	Support to one Response Volunteer in Benin ($10,000) to support malaria activities as well as to support small project grants for malaria for which

65

Proposed Activity	Mechanism	Budget Total $	Budget Commodity $	Geographic Area	Description
					volunteers can submit applications ($10,000).
SUBTOTAL HSS & CAPACITY BUILDING		**$120,000**	**$0**		
BEHAVIOR CHANGE COMMUNICATION					
Support implementation of integrated communication strategy	Community PIHI implementing organizations	$200,000	$0	Selected health zones	Support household visits and group education to promote ITN use, recognizing signs of malaria and increasing care-seeking behavior and encouraging ANC attendance and IPTp through women's groups, CHWs, and mass media.
Technical and financial assistance for national-level communication planning and mass campaigns	New bilateral	$35,000	$0	National	Plan and deliver national malaria events and strategic campaigns.
Technical assistance to strengthen BCC measurement	New bilateral	$25,000	$0	National	Technical assistance to strengthen national efforts to evaluate and document malaria BCC interventions.
SUBTOTAL BCC		**$260,000**	**$0**		
MONITORING AND EVALUATION					
Support RMIS	NMCP	$250,000	$0	National	RMIS strengthening including production of quarterly RMIS bulletin, data quality assurance, maintenance of the database, and a data manager.
PMI Impact Evaluation	New bilateral	$100,000	$0	National	Funding to gather data and provide TA for PMI impact evaluation.

Proposed Activity	Mechanism	Budget		Geographic Area	Description
		Total $	Commodity $		
Conduct EUV surveys	SIAPS	$100,000	$0	National	Monitoring of availability and utilization of key antimalarial commodities at the health facility level.
Technical assistance for M&E	CDC IAA	$10,000	$0	National	Support for one visit by CDC advisor to provide technical assistance for ongoing M&E activities.
SUBTOTAL M&E		$460,000	$0		
IN-COUNTRY STAFFING AND ADMINISTRATION					
CDC	CDC IAA	$378,000	$0	Cotonou	Support for one CDC PMI Advisor.
USAID	USAID	$1,612,048	$0	Cotonou	Support for one USAID PMI Advisor, cross-cutting staff, and other administrative local costs to USAID Mission.
SUBTOTAL IN-COUNTRY STAFFING		$1,990,048	$0		
GRAND TOTAL		$16,500,000	$9,592,952